M000027962

THE
LONDON
POCKET BIBLE

THE POCKET BIBLE SERIES

ACKNOWLEDGEMENTS

I would like to thank Steven (the other team member) for all the love and belief in me. Thanks to my crazy family who are always there for me.

Thanks to Holly Ivins for being a constantly cheerful voice on the end of the phone and for all her encouragement, and to my friend Felicity Whittle (my fellow Blue Badge Guide) for all the fact-checking and help.

Most of all my thanks goes to the wonderful city of London which constantly intrigues and amazes me and makes me realise how privileged I am as a London Blue Badge Guide to be able to tell people about it.

CONTENTS

INTRODUCTION

'No, Sir, when a man is tired of London, he is tired of life;
for there is in London all that life can afford.'
Samuel Johnson

For many of us, London is sometimes an overwhelming city, with so much to see and do, and so many stories to tell, that you do not know where to start. This book will give you all of the necessary information you need about one of the most vibrant and interesting cities in the world. It is a city full of history, architecture, shopping, restaurants, museums, culture and ceremonies. And if that is not enough, there is the darker side of London – with executions, gangsters, murder and tales of ghosts. This city has nearly 2,000 years of history with a wealth of stories just waiting to be told.

If you are a resident of the city, this book will give insight into places that you may have just walked past without even knowing they were there. It will whet your appetite to start discovering a city that you thought you knew.

If you are planning a visit to London, this book will highlight the best places to explore and provide some background to the culture, fashion and the icons that make up this great city. It will help you feel like you really know the city before you start to explore it.

So, whether you are visiting for the first time or looking to find out more about the city you love, this book will provide all of the essential information you need to get to grips with the capital city and all of the fascinating facets which go into making it such an incredible place.

LONDON HISTORY

For nearly 2,000 years London has been the power house of Britain. Like a phoenix from the ashes it has risen again and again following invasions, plague, fires and bombings. The history is fascinating and turbulent, and it has made it the city we see today with medieval churches, warren-like streets and magnificent modern architecture. Here are some of the major events which have shaped the city and its people.

🚗 ROMAN LONDON 🚗

In 55 BC Julius Caesar invaded England, but it wasn't until AD 43 that the Romans truly settled in London. They founded Londonium on the north side of the river, as this area had good anchorage and easy access to their trade routes. It was also sufficiently narrow to build a bridge to the south side. In AD 60 London was burned to the ground by the local tribe and their warrior queen, Boudicca, but the Romans defeated her and rebuilt a magnificent stone city consisting of a forum (marketplace), basilica (government buildings), bathhouses, shops, warehouses, temples and amphitheatre.

Roman ruins you can see in London today

- *Amphitheatre: Guildhall Art Gallery.*
- *Temple of Mithras: Walbrook.*
- *Roman Wall: outside Tower Hill tube, Coopers Row and London Wall.*
- *Roman fort, built in AD 110: Noble Street.*
- *Roman pavement: St Bride's church, Fleet Street.*

- *Museum of London: Ceramics, coins, glass, wood, marble and leatherwork, mosaic floor and western gate of the Roman Wall.*

By AD 200 the city was enclosed by a defensive wall, with six city gates, creating a walled area of around a square mile. Today this square mile is the City's financial district and is still referred to as the 'Square Mile'. Its boundary is guarded by the emblem of the City of London, two silver dragons holding a shield decorated with the Cross of St George (see p.50 for more on this).

City gates

The old Roman gates no longer exist but the following locations still bear their medieval names:

- *Aldgate*
- *Newgate*
- *Ludgate*
- *Cripplegate*
- *Aldersgate*
- *Bishopsgate*

By AD 410 the Roman empire was beginning to crumble and Rome itself was being threatened by the Germanic tribes. It became necessary to withdraw the legions from England, and London had to try to defend itself from foreign invaders after 350 years of Roman rule.

Pocket Fact

Today the City of London is about 20ft above the old Roman City, so developers sometimes have to allow archaeologists full access to the site when digging foundations for new buildings.

🚌 ANGLO-SAXON LONDON 🚌

Without the protection of Rome, London was just an invasion waiting to happen. The Anglo-Saxons who invaded and settled after the Romans were a mixture of tribes; the Angles were southern Danish, the Saxons, Franks and Frisians were German-Dutch and the Jutes were northern Danish. It is from the Angles that we get the name England.

The Anglo-Saxons established a settlement called Lundenwic around a mile from the Roman city and from the 9th century started to occupy the abandoned city of London. For the next 600 years a mixture of Danes, Vikings and Saxons ruled London.

ANGLO-SAXON LONDON TIMELINE

- **AD 410**: Anglo-Saxons establish Lundenwic.
- **AD 842**: Vikings attack and occupy London. At the time it was described as the 'Great Slaughter' as they killed many of the inhabitants.
- **AD 886**: London recaptured by Anglo-Saxon Alfred of Wessex, later to be King Alfred.
- **1013**: King Ethelred, descendant of Alfred, flees the Danish King Sweyn but returns after Sweyn dies.
- **1016**: King Edmund, son of Ethelred, cedes London to Danish King Cnut.
- **1042**: King Cnut dies and the throne reverts to Edward, the surviving son of Ethelred.
- **1065**: Edward the Confessor builds the Abbey of St Peter and a palace at Westminster but is too weak to attend the consecration. He dies 10 days later and is buried in the Abbey.

Myths & Legends 🚌

In 1163 Edward the Confessor was created a saint and it is said that his body is perfectly preserved in Westminster Abbey.

🚗 NORMAN LONDON 🚗

The next event to have a significant impact on the shape of London was in 1066, at the battle of Hastings, when William the Conqueror, Duke of Normandy, defeated King Harold, who had succeeded Edward the Confessor. William knew he had to conquer London so he laid waste to the surrounding countryside. The city's leading men were concerned that William would destroy London, so they surrendered to him and invited him to be King. William was crowned at Westminster Abbey on Christmas Day in 1066.

Pocket Fact 🌉

Every coronation since William the Conqueror in 1066 (apart from Edward V and Edward VIII) has taken place at Westminster Abbey; a total of 38 coronations.

BUILDING THE TOWER OF LONDON

William the Conqueror wanted to demonstrate his power and prestige to the London population and so he built the Tower of London. What better way to demonstrate his new power than to construct a building the size of which the city had never seen before. With its walls 118ft high and 13ft thick, the tower dominated the London skyline and also the hearts and minds of the subjugated London population (see p.18 for more on the Tower).

Even then the English did not learn French!

Under William the Conqueror the ruling Norman classes spoke French while the Saxon population still spoke English. This created differences in the English language that still exist today. The Saxons tended the livestock and the Normans ate the meat, and that is why we have:

On the table	*In the field*
Beef/Boeuf	*Cow*
Pork/Porc	*Pig*
Mutton/Mouton	*Sheep*

DEVELOPMENT OF THE CITY OF WESTMINSTER

Westminster continued to be developed as the area of government under the Normans, when William Rufus, the son of William the Conqueror, built Westminster Hall as part of the Royal Palace of Westminster. It was the largest hall in Europe, 239ft long and 67ft wide, and as such represented his power. It was used for ceremonial banquets and feasting and it was here that the King's principal throne stood.

🚗 12TH-CENTURY LONDON 🚗

- **1135**: King Stephen: a fire destroys a large part of London in 1135 and the partially built St Paul's Cathedral.

- **1176**: Henry II: building of the first stone London Bridge begins.

- **1189**: Richard I (The Lion-Heart): after spending most of his time fighting the Crusades in the Holy Land and desperate for money to continue fighting, Richard is known to have said 'I would sell London if I could find a buyer'.

🚗 13TH-CENTURY LONDON 🚗

- **1215**: John: the Barons rebel and gain control of the Tower of London forcing John to sign the Magna Carta, establishing the fundamental rights of the people in Britain.

Several clauses of the Magna Carta are still used today including:

- The guarantee of the freedom of the English Church.

- The confirmation and guarantee of the rights and privileges of the city of London.

- That no free man shall be imprisoned, dispossessed, outlawed or exiled without the lawful judgment of his equals or by the law of the land known as habeas corpus.

ENLARGING THE TOWER OF LONDON AND BUILDING WESTMINSTER ABBEY

Given the problems his father had with the barons, Henry III decided to enlarge and reinforce the Tower of London in 1220. He also built beautifully decorated lodgings for himself and his queen, Eleanor of Provence, within the tower. He painted the tower white, giving it the name the White Tower.

Pocket Fact ⚔️

The Tower zoo started with a diplomatic gift of three leopards to Henry III. Subsequent gifts included a polar bear that caught fish in the Thames while chained to the bank, an elephant, the first to be seen in Britain, and an ostrich which died from being fed nails in the mistaken belief that it could digest iron.

At the same time, Henry, who was known as the 'Builder King', laid the foundation stone to build a new magnificent Westminster Abbey dedicated to Edward the Confessor. It would be built in the new Gothic style and replace the old abbey built by Edward. Henry built a magnificent new shrine for St Edward and when he died, he was buried in the abbey that he built.

The 17 monarchs buried in Westminster Abbey

Edward the Confessor	*Richard II*
Henry III	*Henry V*
Edward I	*Henry VII*
Edward III	*Edward VI*

Mary Tudor　　　　　*William III*
Elizabeth I　　　　　*Mary II*
James I　　　　　　　*Anne*
Mary, Queen of Scots　*George II*
Charles II

🚗 14TH-CENTURY LONDON 🚗

- **1348**: Edward III: the plague or 'Black Death' reaches London, killing over 17,000 people. Record-keeping was very poor at the time and modern historians think the death toll could actually have been up to 500,000.

- **1377**: Richard II: Westminster Hall is repaired by Richard. The walls are made higher and new roof constructed and the Guildhall, the home of the City of London's government is built.

- **1381**: Richard II: Peasants from Kent and Essex march on London to revolt over the unfair tax system. The leaders are eventually captured and executed on Tower Hill.

- **1399**: Henry IV: Henry becomes king when his cousin Richard II is captured, imprisoned in the Tower of London and forced to renounce his throne.

THE CITY LIVERY COMPANIES AND DICK WHITTINGTON

During this period the City livery companies, which governed and represented trade, had confirmed their status by building magnificent halls and holding wonderful processions through the city. It was from the livery company of Mercers, dealers in valuable cloth, that Richard II imposed Richard Whittington as Lord Mayor in 1397. Richard Whittington negotiated a return of the city's liberties, one of which was that the city could choose its own mayor. He was then successfully elected as mayor four months later. He was Lord Mayor of London four times and became extremely wealthy, although he donated much of his wealth to good causes and the rebuilding of the Guildhall.

Myths & Legends 🚌

The famous pantomime character Dick Whittington is based on Richard Whittington, but he was not a poor orphan boy as seen in the pantomime. In fact, he came from a well-off Gloucestershire family. It is not known if he had a cat (although it was common to own one at the time because of the rat population) but he was married to Alice Fitzwarren. He is buried in St Michael Paternoster Royal and is commemorated by a window with a picture of a cat.

🚕 15TH-CENTURY LONDON 🚕

- **1413**: Henry V: a huge banquet and procession take place in London when Henry returns in triumph from his great victory over the French at the battle of Agincourt in 1415.

- **1422–1461**: Henry VI: the city supports Edward IV in the Wars of the Roses and escapes any upheaval.

- **1471**: Henry VI dies in the Tower of London during the Wars of the Roses, leaving Edward free to rule. It is said that Henry died of 'pure displeasure and melancholy', but in reality he was stabbed to death and the culprit was never found.

- **1486**: Henry VII marries Elizabeth of York in Westminster Abbey uniting the warring Lancaster and York families and beginning a new royal dynasty, the Tudors.

🚕 16TH-CENTURY LONDON 🚕

- **1503–1509**: Henry VII: Henry completes Westminster Abbey by building the Lady Chapel at the east end of the abbey, where he is buried with his wife, Elizabeth of York.

- **1509**: Henry VIII: royal dockyards are built at Woolwich and Deptford.

- **1534**: Henry VIII: Parliament passes the Act of Supremacy that creates Henry VIII as the Supreme Head of the new

Church of England, allowing him to divorce his first wife Catherine of Aragon and marry Anne Boleyn, in the hope that she would give him a son and heir. The marriage doesn't last, as only three years later Henry orders Anne's execution.

Pocket Fact

The armour in the Tower of London shows how Henry VIII's figure changed over the years from a virile, athletic man with a 42-inch chest and 35-inch waist to a very large 57-inch chest and a 54-inch waist.

- **1547**: Edward VI: Christ's Hospital school is founded at Newgate to replace the monastic school for the poor destroyed by Edward's father.

- **1554**: Mary I: Thomas Wyatt marches on London with 4,000 men. The rebellion ends at Ludgate Hill and Wyatt is imprisoned in the Tower of London and hanged, drawn and quartered on Tower Hill.

- **1558**: Elizabeth I: Shakespeare comes to London and the Queen approves the building of theatres on the south bank of the Thames.

🚗 17TH-CENTURY LONDON 🚗

THE GUNPOWDER PLOT

After Elizabeth I died childless and James VI of Scotland took the throne to become James I of England, the Catholics hoped that James would restore the Catholic Church in England, but this was not to be. Several plots were hatched to remove the King but none came as close as the Gunpowder Plot on 5 November 1605.

There were five main plotters including Guy Fawkes, who planned to blow up James I in the Houses of Parliament in protest at the expulsion of the Jesuits and Catholic priests. The plotters rented a house nearby and smuggled 36 barrels of gunpowder into the cellars of the Houses of Parliament through a tunnel. Luckily, the plot was discovered as the cellars were searched on 4 November. They found Guy Fawkes ready to light the fuse the next day when the King and Parliament were seated. A day of celebration and thanksgiving was ordered by the King, to be marked by bonfires, while Guy Fawkes and his fellow plotters were executed.

Pocket Fact ⚉

The cellars are still ceremonially searched each year before the annual opening of Parliament.

- **1608**: James I: the first recorded Frost Fair takes place on the frozen River Thames including football matches, ice bowling, food stalls and taverns.

- **1625**: Charles I: Covent Garden is developed by the Earl of Bedford and is the first example of London town planning and the first public square in the country.

- **1642**: Charles I: Charles attempts to arrest Pym, the leader of the Long Parliament, marking the beginning of the English Civil War.

- **1647**: Charles I: Charles hands himself over to the Scottish Presbyterians, who surrender him to Parliament. He is tried for treason at Westminster Hall for waging war on his own people, for being a tyrant and a traitor, and is found guilty.

- **1648**: Oliver Cromwell becomes Lord Protector. Under Cromwell, London is forced to follow strict Puritan beliefs which means many activities, such as the theatre, Christmas celebrations, make-up and colourful dresses are banned. Cromwell also orders all theatres and playhouses to be pulled down, including the Globe theatre.

- **1649**: Charles I is executed. It is bitterly cold and Charles wears two heavy shirts so that he will not shiver and let the crowd think he was afraid. One of the last things he sees as he leaves Whitehall is the ceiling he had commissioned celebrating the monarchy and Stuart dynasty.

- **1660**: Restoration of the monarchy: King Charles II returns as the monarch, and a new set of coronation regalia, including a new crown, is made for his coronation as Cromwell had melted down or sold the crown jewels. The only item to survive is the 12th-century anointing spoon, which is used to anoint the monarch with holy oil.

Pocket Fact 🌉

The Crown Jewels at the Tower of London contain some of the most spectacular diamonds and precious stones. The most famous diamond is the Cullinan I which was found in the Cullinan mine in South Africa. It sits in the Royal Sceptre, is 536 carats (about the size of a fist) and was cut from the largest stone ever found (3,106 carats).

- **1665**: Charles II: in April 1665, following a mild winter that fails to control the rat population responsible for spreading the plague, an epidemic breaks out exceeding all previous ones. In July 17,000 die, and in August 31,000 die. By the time the outbreak is over in 1666 around 100,000 people are dead.

1666 FIRE OF LONDON

On 2 September 1666 London was to suffer yet another major disaster. In the early hours of the morning, the embers of a fire in a bake house in Pudding Lane provided a spark that was to devastate the old medieval city.

It had been a hot, dry summer and the dry timber houses were just waiting to be consumed by the fire. Warehouses were full of fuel for the coming winter including tobacco, sugar and gunpowder. A strong wind fanned the flames as the fire leapt from house to house in the narrow streets. The King, Charles II, ordered houses to be pulled down to create a fire break to stop the fire spreading.

The fire raged for four days and while it has always been said that the death toll was very low, estimated at just nine people, the heat of the fire would have incinerated bodies and so the current thinking is that the number could be in the hundreds or even thousands. Nearly four-fifths of the City was destroyed by the fire, including 87 churches together with St Paul's, 44 halls of the livery companies and 13,000 houses, which left 100,000 people homeless. During the fire:

- Pigeons fell from the sky on fire as there was nowhere to land.

- The lead from St Paul's Cathedral melted and ran in rivers down the street.

- The metal bars of Newgate prison melted.

- The Tower of London was saved by blowing up the surrounding houses.

- There was no night as the fire lit up the sky as if it was daytime.

Myths & Legends 🚌

The fire was considered to be a punishment for the gluttony of Londoners because it started in Pudding Lane and finished at Pye Corner.

After the fire, Charles II called for plans to replace the old city with a new one with wide boulevards and grand vistas. Some streets were widened and the first pavements were built. But Charles's great scheme never happened as Londoners rushed back to reclaim their plots of land and rebuild the city on the same medieval footprint.

- **1694**: the Bank of England is founded.

🚌 18TH-CENTURY LONDON 🚌

- **1700s**: London's population explodes from 200,000 in 1600 to 600,000 by 1707 (the next largest city is Edinburgh with 35,000). As the centre of everything fashionable, rich people begin to come to London for 'the season' (Easter to August) looking for entertainment and to spend money on the latest clothes, books and the theatre. As Westminster and the surrounding areas grow, the City becomes less residential and more business orientated, emerging as the financial and credit capital.

Tale of two cities

London is divided into two cities, the City of London and the City of Westminster. The City of London is nearly 2,000 years old and was founded by the Romans, while the City of Westminster was developed in the 11th century and became the centre of royal power and the government. The best way to remember the difference between the two is that the City makes the money as the financial district and Westminster spends it as the political and entertainment district.

- **1714**: George I: gin drinking, known as 'Mother's Ruin', becomes extremely popular among London's poor. It is seen as the cause of debauchery and immoral behaviour.

- **1739**: George II: Captain Coram establishes the Foundling hospital as a place for destitute mothers to leave their babies.

- **1780**: George III: Lord Gordon leads a crowd of 50,000 to Westminster to protest against the 1778 Roman Catholic Relief Act allowing Catholics greater freedoms. The rioters destroy Catholic churches, Newgate Prison and damage several buildings including the Bank of England. The army is called in and 285 rioters are killed and 200 wounded.

🚗 19TH-CENTURY LONDON 🚗

- **1820**: George IV: the first horse-drawn London omnibus begins service provided by Mr George Shillibeer, and carries up to 22 passengers between Paddington and Bank.

- **1830**: George IV: London, the capital of 'the empire where the sun never set', is transformed and its industrial might is reflected in the introduction of the first railway, the first underground railway from Paddington to Euston and King's Cross and the new dock area built in East London.

Pocket Fact ⚓

Victorian stations still in use today:

Cannon Street	Blackfriars	London Bridge
Euston	Victoria	Fenchurch Street
King's Cross	St Pancras	Charing Cross
Paddington	Liverpool Street	Marylebone

🚗 20TH-CENTURY LONDON 🚗

- **1901**: Edward VII: the first London Olympic Games are held at White City in 1908.

- **1915**: George V: the first German air raids take place in London during the First World War.

- **1948**: George VI: the second London Olympic Games are held at Wembley stadium.

THE BLITZ

The London Blitz during the Second World War lasted for 76 nights, from September 1940 to May 1941. The Germans thought that they could bomb London into submission. On the first night, over 300 bombers dropped high explosives and incendiary devices onto the city. They focused particularly on the Port of London and East London where ships came into the dock areas to deliver supplies and where the warehouses stored goods and food. The Germans hoped that without these vital supplies Londoners would just give up or starve.

Pocket Fact ▟▛▙

The Firefighters Memorial, commemorating the effort of the fire service during the Blitz, is located at City Walkway.

Westminster was also bombed, but not with the same intensity as many of its buildings were meant for commercial and entertainment use. However, Soho, Millbank and Pimlico were residential areas and bombs dropped there wiped out whole families. The total number of civilian deaths in London was 30,000, but 1.4 million people were made homeless and the City of London was never to be a residential area again. Today only around 8,000 people live there.

Some facts about the Blitz

- *The blackout meant there were no street lights, houses had blackout curtains to prevent any light showing, there were no lights in Piccadilly Circus and car lights were reduced to slits.*
- *The worst raid was on 29 December 1940, starting 1,400 fires.*
- *Incendiary bombs caused the most damage. They were dropped in clusters and filled with a highly inflammable liquid which ignited on impact.*
- *Warehouses full of rum, sugar, paint and spirits were bombed, creating a river of burning molten liquid.*
- *The ash from the fires was so bad that the firemen said it looked like a snow storm.*
- *People got used to the raids and went to the theatre and cinema despite the bombs falling.*

When the Blitz came to an end in 1941, the area between St Mary le Bow and St Paul's Cathedral had been reduced to ruins. By some miracle St Paul's Cathedral, a building which came to represent the strength of Londoners, survived. After one particularly bad night of bombing, when it looked as if fire might consume the building, Churchill redirected the fire services to St Paul's and said that it was to 'be saved at all costs'.

Pocket Fact 🚋

Each night during the blitz 40 people from the St Paul's Watch protected the great cathedral. Climbing in the roof at night they either put the incendiary bombs in a bucket of sand to prevent them from igniting or doused the fire before it took hold.

🚗 MODERN LONDON 🚗

- **1956**: The traditional view of London covered in a dramatic fog (actually smog), which many authors and artists had used to their advantage, comes to an end with the introduction of the Clean Air Act, banning the burning of dirty coal.

- **1960s**: The youth-orientated city (over half the population was under 30) becomes a hotbed of new music and fashion focusing on the young. Carnaby Street and Chelsea are the places to be seen in miniskirts and hotpants.

- **1979**: The Jubilee line, the last underground line to be built, opens.

- **1987**: The Canadian Reichman brothers sign a deal to develop the 29 hectares of Canary Wharf, one area of the old Georgian docks in East London, now known as Docklands. Around 300,000 men had worked at the docks but with the introduction of container shipping, the area fell into disuse in the 1960s. The intention was to attract companies out of the crowded and expensive area of the City of London with cheaper rents and nearby facilities, like shops, bars, restaurants, a cinema, good transport links and a cheaper residential area. Now 90,000 people work in this area.

Pocket Fact 🌉

Canary Wharf is so called because imported fruit such as oranges, lemons and bananas from the Canary Islands were unloaded there.

THE 2012 OLYMPICS

On the 6 July 2005, people held their breath waiting for the decision of the International Olympic Committee (IOC). When Jacques Rogge, President of the IOC, announced the result there was a huge cheer from the bid committee and the people waiting in Trafalgar Square and Stratford. The Olympics and Paralympics were coming to London after a wait of 64 years.

Pocket Fact 🌉

The Olympic Park, which will become Queen Elizabeth Park after the games, will have the postcode E20, currently used by the fictional EastEnders borough of Walford.

The Olympic Park covers an area of 500 acres in East London, between the boroughs of Newham, Waltham Forest, Hackney and Tower Hamlets and the lower Lea Valley. It was one of the largest regeneration projects in Britain, including miles of waterways. See p.128 for more on the Olympics in London.

London – the tourist capital of the world

- *Over 14 million tourists visit London per year.*
- *The British Museum is the top tourist attraction, with 5.5 million visitors.*
- *Americans make the most visits at 1.7 million.*
- *London tourism brings in £8.3 billion of revenue.*
- *In 2008 London topped the Euromonitor International's Top City Destinations.*

2

LONDON ARCHITECTURE

The variety of London architecture is amazing; where else could you find the Tower of London, a medieval castle, on one side of the river and the Greater London Authority headquarters, an ultra-modern glass building, on the other. London's buildings are as numerous as they are diverse and fascinating and over the last 1,000 years a number of styles have been used. London has many wonderful and stunning buildings and three of them, the Tower of London, Maritime Greenwich, and Westminster Abbey and the Palace of Westminster are UNESCO World Heritage Sites. This chapter profiles seven buildings which are iconic symbols of London, as well as looking at some of the most famous London hotels and the unique statues that can be found all over the capital.

🚗 TOWER OF LONDON 🚗

The Tower on the north bank of the Thames on Tower Hill Terrace. Built by William the Conqueror from Kentish Ragstone and Caen stone shipped from William's native France, the Tower has been an imposing sight for nearly 1,000 years.

The beautiful St John's Chapel in the Tower with its heavy round columns and Romanesque arches is one of the few remaining examples of Anglo-Norman architecture in London.

The Tower was never intended to be a royal palace but a fortress where the King could go if the city was under attack. In the early 13th century, concerned about rebellion in his kingdom, King

Henry III fortified the Tower by surrounding it with an encircling wall, adding nine additional towers and a moat on three sides (the fourth side was protected by the Thames).

Henry's son Edward I continued his father's building programme by creating a new moat, and building another lower wall to encircle the existing wall with a new tower that contained additional living accommodation. It is this layout, a perfect example of a concentric castle, which created the formidable fortification we see today.

Pocket Fact ⚓

During the 19th century, the Constable of the Tower, the Duke of Wellington, closed off the moat built by Edward I because the water was smelly.

The long history of the Tower is still reflected by its various features:

- Elaborately carved into the Beauchamp Tower walls are the names and inscriptions of its prisoners, including Lady Jane Grey, the nine-day Queen (see p.137).

- Queen's House is on Tower Green, from where Anne Boleyn took her last walk to the executioner's block. This is also the site of the church of St Peter Vincula, where she was laid to rest.

- The Wakefield Tower houses an exhibition of torture, showing terrible instruments such as a replica of the rack.

- The Wellington Barracks contain the Crown Jewels, a magnificent collection of 23,578 diamonds and precious stones set into a number of crowns. They include the Coronation Crown only ever removed from the Tower for the coronation and the Imperial State Crown, which has 2,868 diamonds, 273 pearls, 17 sapphires, 11 emeralds and five rubies.

- The yeoman warders still guard the Tower as they have done for the past 700 years.

🚗 TOWER BRIDGE 🚗

Tower Bridge is the most famous bridge in London and the one that everyone wants to be photographed with. It was built in 1894, next to the Tower of London, to provide an additional crossing over the river Thames to ease the traffic congestion over London Bridge, proving that traffic jams are not a modern invention!

The upper walkways on the bridge were closed in 1910 as they were popular with prostitutes and pickpockets.

The design of the bridge had to blend with the Tower of London as well as allowing tall ships to pass through the bridge. Over 50 designs were submitted for the competition to design the bridge. Horace Jones won the competition but unfortunately died before it was completed. George D. Stevenson completed the design of the bridge and added some of the Gothic flourishes and stone cladding.

Pocket Fact ⌁

In 1952 a relief watchman forgot to sound the warning bell that the bridge was opening. The bridge started to open just as a number 78 double-decker bus was crossing, so the driver stuck his foot on the accelerator and just managed to jump the gap.

TOWER BRIDGE DESIGN FEATURES

- The towers are nearly 120ft high and constructed from steel and clad in stone.

- The opening of the bridge was originally steam powered but today it is powered by electricity.

- There are two walkways at the top of the bridge which allowed pedestrians to cross even when the bridge was open. These walkways now house the Tower Bridge exhibition.

- When the bridge was first built it opened up to 6,000 times per year. Now it opens around once or twice a day and 24 hours' notice is required.

🚗 GREENWICH 🚗

Greenwich is home to a wonderful collection of buildings, including the Queen's House, designed by Inigo Jones, and the Royal Naval College, the Royal Observatory and the National Maritime Museum.

Greenwich sits on the most eastern approach to London and is best visited by river bus.

Pocket Tip ❗

Visit the Transport of London website (www.tfl.gov.uk/ gettingaround/15544.aspx) for bus times and stops.

THE ROYAL NAVAL COLLEGE

The Royal Naval College was established by royal charter in 1694. Queen Mary II employed Christopher Wren to design a hospital for the relief and support of 3,000 seamen. When Wren retired, his Baroque design was completed by various architects including Nicholas Hawksmoor, John Vanburgh and James 'Athenian' Stuart. In 1869 the number of seamen needing help declined, so the hospital was used as a Naval College until 1997 when it was leased as one of three campuses for Greenwich University.

Pocket Fact 🌉

In Greenwich you can stand on the world-famous Greenwich meridian, the prime meridian of the world: longitude 0 degrees.

ARCHITECTURAL GEMS IN GREENWICH

- Greenwich is home to a quaint market and shops, as well as the church of St Alfege, one of the finest Nicholas Hawksmoor churches built in 1714 on the site of the 11th century martyrdom of St Alfege.

- The Painted Hall in the Royal Naval College was painted by James Thornhill between 1707 and 1727. He was paid by the foot to decorate the walls and ceiling of the sailors' dining room.

- The Royal Observatory was used as such until 1960, when the observatory transferred to Herstmonceux in East Sussex. Today you can still see the refracting telescope built in 1893, the largest of its kind in Britain, and you can still see the stars, as in 2007 the observatory opened a planetarium.

- The National Maritime Museum was opened by George VI in 1937 and holds a huge collection of artefacts tracing Britain's naval history.

Pocket Fact 🌉

Nelson's coat from the Battle of Trafalgar is on display in the National Maritime Museum. There is a hole in the left shoulder, created by the bullet that mortally wounded him.

🚖 WESTMINSTER ABBEY 🚖

The Anglican church, Westminster Abbey, or to give it its official name 'The Collegiate Church of St Peter at Westminster', is in the heart of London's political district near Parliament Square.

Pocket Fact 🌉

Westminster Abbey is known as the royal church because since 1066 every coronation has taken place here.

This outstanding church with its high ceilings and pointed arches is one of the finest examples of Gothic architecture in London built by King Henry III in 1245. In the 12th century the French devised a way of building tall churches without the walls falling outwards, and Westminster Abbey is a fine example of this method of building with its large columns and pointed arches to support the ceiling. The flying buttresses on the outside act like a rib cage to support the walls. Because the walls were no longer load-bearing, the abbey could have large stained glass windows with elegant tracery.

Although it was built over a period of 300 years the kings responsible kept the same style of architecture and building materials. The only difference is the strikingly beautiful Lady Chapel built by Henry VII in the 16th century, which is in the later Gothic Perpendicular style; a style which was more decorative than the early Gothic architecture.

Pocket Fact

The gravestone of Ben Jonson, the famous 16th-century writer, is just 2ft by 2ft because he could not afford a full length grave, and so was buried standing up.

WESTMINSTER ABBEY HIGHLIGHTS

- There are 3,000 gravestones and memorials located here. Geoffrey Chaucer, Charles Dickens and Thomas Hardy are buried in the famous Poets' Corner, and you can also find the graves of the scientists Sir Isaac Newton and Charles Darwin, and musicians such as Henry Purcell and Vaughan Williams.

- The 14th-century coronation chair sits waiting to be taken down for the next coronation. The last time it was used was in 1953 when 8,000 people crowded into the abbey to see the coronation of Elizabeth II.

- The tomb of the Unknown Soldier is the only grave that is never walked on. The funeral of the Unknown Soldier took place on 11 November 1920.

HOUSES OF PARLIAMENT

The Houses of Parliament (or the Palace of Westminster as it is known) stands on the north bank of the Thames, situated opposite Westminster Abbey in Parliament Square, covering an area of eight acres. The view of the architecture of the Houses of Parliament from the south bank of the Thames is stunning. From here you can see all the ornamental stonework and Gothic pinnacles in all their glory.

It was the close proximity to Westminster Abbey that greatly influenced its style of architecture. In October 1834 a fire destroyed nearly all of the Old Palace, a number of medieval buildings which had been the home of Parliament. After the fire, a competition was held specifying that the new buildings were to be Gothic or Elizabethan in design. Charles Barry was the winner from 97 entries and chose Perpendicular Gothic to match the outside of the Lady Chapel of Westminster Abbey. The foundation stone for the building was laid in 1840.

Pocket Fact ◢━━▟

A portcullis (latticed gate) topped with a crown is the symbol of the Houses of Parliament and appears on the chairs, stationery, cutlery, silver and china. The portcullis symbol came into use in 1512 during the rebuilding of the Old Palace after a fire. It was the badge adopted by Henry VII from his mother Margaret Beaufort.

The inside of the building was a collaboration between Charles Barry and Augustus Pugin, who submitted drawings for every part of the building, even down to the chairs. The interiors of the building are stunning; every surface is decorated, some with historical themes and there are statues, wood carvings and paintings depicting historical scenes.

The building is divided into two distinct sections, the House of Commons, where the Members of Parliament work, and House of Lords, where the appointed upper House of Lords work.

HOUSES OF PARLIAMENT HIGHLIGHTS

- The Victoria Tower is 323ft and sits over the sovereign entrance which the monarch uses at the State Opening of Parliament.

- The House of Lords interior is the most lavishly decorated room in red and gold. Between the windows are statues of the 16 barons and the two bishops known to have been present at the Magna Carta in 1215.

- There are over 1,100 rooms and 100 staircases arranged around a series of courtyards.

BIG BEN

The most recognisable part of the building is the Clock Tower and clock, while the most recognisable sound is that of Big Ben, the 13-ton bell which hangs in the Clock Tower and strikes the number of hours.

Pocket Fact 🌉

The name 'Big Ben' either comes from Sir Benjamin Hall, who was the commissioner of works, or a famous boxer of the mid-19th century, Benjamin Caunt.

Big Ben highlights

- The tower is 319ft tall and it is possible to take a tour up the tower to the clock (see below).

- The clock faces are 23ft across and were shattered in 1941 by a German bomb. The hour hands are 8.5ft long and the numbers 2ft high.

- Timing is maintained by adding or subtracting pre-decimal pennies to the pendulum, adding one penny adds 2/5 second.

- Tours of the Palace of Westminster can be arranged either by contacting your local Member of Parliament or by purchasing a ticket for the tours that take place every Saturday or during the summer recess in August and September. Tours which climb the clock tower must be arranged through your Member of Parliament or a member of the House of Lords.

ST PAUL'S CATHEDRAL

This magnificent Anglican English Baroque cathedral designed by Christopher Wren is the fourth cathedral to occupy this site on Ludgate Hill. Baroque architecture began in Italy and Wren adopted its style to create the wonderful dome, columns, pediment and stone carvings of flowers, fruit and cherubs that adorn St Paul's Cathedral. The dome is one of the most famous sights in the London skyline as it rises majestically above the surrounding buildings.

King Charles II commissioned Wren to design a new St Paul's after the Fire of London in 1666. It took 35 years to build and was completed in 1710. The Warrant design was approved by the king, but there was a clause that allowed Wren to make any changes he deemed necessary. Wren took full advantage of this clause and changed the Warrant design as the cathedral was being built.

The principal changes Wren made to the Warrant design meant:

- The space under the dome was emphasised.

- The upper part of the cathedral has a handsome two-storey exterior façade.

- A tall dome was raised over the crossing.

Whereas Westminster Abbey is the royal church, St Paul's is the people's church. It is here that the people of London come to commemorate and celebrate, including events such as the Diamond Jubilee of Queen Victoria, peace services marking the end of The First and Second World Wars, the Golden Jubilee and the 80th birthday of Queen Elizabeth II. The state funerals of Admiral Nelson, Duke of Wellington and Winston Churchill all took place here. The royal wedding of Prince Charles and Lady Diana also took place here because Westminster Abbey was considered too small.

Pocket Fact 🌉

Christopher Wren's tomb is surprisingly modest but the inscription under the dome says it all: 'O Reader, if you seek his monument look around you'.

ST PAUL'S CATHEDRAL HIGHLIGHTS

- The dome is 365ft high, and the first 257 steps lead up to the Whispering Gallery, where if you whisper on one side the person on the other side can hear. The next 376 steps take you to the stone gallery and splendid views over London, while after another 528 steps you arrive at the Golden Gallery, the highest point of the dome.

- The mosaics that decorate the area under the dome and up to the altar were installed in the late 1800s after Queen Victoria complained that the inside was very dull.

- The American chapel was paid for by public donations and commemorates the thousands of American servicemen and -women who were killed during the Second World War. The chapel was built after the east end of the church was damaged by a German bomb.

- The crypt beneath the main church contains the tombs of Wellington and Nelson and memorials to military heroes. It is also the resting place of Christopher Wren.

🚗 THE GHERKIN 🚗

This bullet-shaped building, located in the heart of the City of London's financial district, has several names including the Swiss Re Building and 30 St Mary Axe, but it is most commonly known as 'The Gherkin'.

The Gherkin was commissioned by Swiss Re (a reinsurance company), designed by Norman Foster and completed in 2003 and has since won 11 architecturel prizes. It had been 25 years since

London had a new office tower, and although the design was not very popular at first the Gherkin has quickly become as familiar a London landmark as the dome of St Paul's Cathedral or Big Ben.

The building is clad in 5,500 pieces of flat triangular and diamond shaped glass which varies at each level and would cover five football pitches. This glass reflects the clouds, the sun and the surrounding buildings making the Gherkin as a constantly changing work of art. At night it stands out like a beacon.

THE GHERKIN HIGHLIGHTS

- It is naturally ventilated with air drawn up through spiralling light wells and it is double glazed, thereby reducing the need for air conditioning or central heating. It is said to use only half the energy of a traditional building this size.

- It is 623ft tall, with 40 floors, and on the top floor there is a lounge bar and restaurant for the tenants with 360-degree views of London.

- The remains of a Roman teenage girl were found during construction. They were stored in the Museum of London for 12 years. A service was held for her at St Botolph's church and she was reburied near the Gherkin.

- The shape, which is wider in the middle than at the base, allowed a landscaped area around the building.

- Despite its curved shape there is only one curved piece of glass, the lens-shaped cap on the top.

- Below level 35, the windows are cleaned by men in one or two cradles. Above that, a hydraulic cherry picker is used.

Pocket Fact 🌉

The OXO Tower on the south bank of the Thames was once the cold store for the Oxo Cube Company. The owners weren't allowed to advertise their product on the building so the name appears in the decoration of the three windows at the top of the tower, consisting of a circle, a cross and another circle.

🚗 TOP TEN FAMOUS 🚗
LONDON HOTELS

London is home to some of the most famous and glamorous hotels in the world, all with an impressive history and clientele.

The Ritz

Opened: 1906
Location: Piccadilly

The hotel is famous for its afternoon tea in the Palm Court. One year on Christmas Day, two containers of sea water were brought from Brighton so a guest could have a saltwater bath.

Savoy

Opened: 1889
Location: Strand

Built in Art Nouveau styling in 1889, it was the first hotel to have en-suite bathrooms and electric lights.

Claridges

Opened: 1854
Location: 49 Brook Street

In 1945 Churchill gave permission for one of the rooms to be part of Yugoslavia so the Crown Prince Alexander could be born in Yugoslavia.

The Dorchester

Opened: 1931
Location: Park Lane

In 1938 three of the most famous cocktails were invented here by Harry Craddock – the Martini, Manhattan and White Lady.

The Goring

Opened: 1910
Location: Beeston Place

Run by the same family that built it over 100 years ago The Goring has always been a favourite of the royal family. It was here that the Duchess of Cambridge spent her last night as Catherine Middleton and both the pre-wedding party and wedding reception for the Middleton family and their friends were held here.

The Connaught

Opened: 1901
Location: Carlos Place

Named after the son of Queen Victoria, the Duke of Connaught. Each guest gets their own butler.

Browns

Opened: 1837
Location: Albemarle Street

In 1859 the hotel was owned by Henry Ford, who installed baths, electric lighting and one of the first lifts in Britain.

The Berkeley

Opened: 1972
Location: Wilton Place

Afternoon tea is Prêt-à-Portea, where the cakes are inspired by designers such as Alexander McQueen, Anya Hindmarch and Philip Treacy, and are in the shape of dresses, bags and hats.

The Stafford

Opened: 1858
Location: via Blue Ball Yard, St James's Street

The American bar is fascinating with its eclectic mix of memorabilia. Some of its rooms are in the 18th-century old stables opposite the hotel, now called the Carriage Rooms.

Blakes

Opened: 1986
Location: 33 Roland Gardens

This Anouska Hempel lavishly designed hotel is a favourite with celebrities such as David and Victoria Beckham, Lindsay Lohan, Leonardo DiCaprio, Mickey Rourke and Quentin Tarantino.

Pocket Fact 🌉

One of the most stunning architectural venues in London is the Royal Opera House. When entering the auditorium the audience is dazzled by the hundreds of lights fixed to the balconies. With the red lined boxes of the grand and first tier of seats and the gold saucer-domed ceiling, it is a riot of red and gold.

🚗 LONDON'S BEST STATUES 🚗 OR SCULPTURES

London is home to some unique and quirky statues and sculptures, all of which commemorate a part of the city's fascinating history.

The Battle of Britain Memorial, Embankment

This wonderful sculpture depicts the people who helped win the Battle of Britain including pilots, women working in the factories and mechanics. Look out for the man trying to steal a kiss!

Wellington on his horse, Hyde Park Corner

This lovely statue of the Duke of Wellington on his favourite horse Copenhagen was built to commemorate Britain's victory over Napoleon at the Battle of Waterloo.

Animals in War Memorial, Park Lane

This memorial has statues of a horse, mules and a dog, plus animals engraved on the flanking walls to commemorate the contribution made by animals during the conflicts in the 20th century.

The Giant Plug, Ganton Street

A modern sculpture, this giant electrical socket and plug on the façade of an electricity substation lights up at night in a variety of colours.

Charlie Chaplin, Leicester Square

The bronze statue of Charlie Chaplin stands in the centre of London's film premiere district and commemorates the fact that he was born in London's East End.

The Crutched Friars statues, Crutched Friars

The office block now standing here is built on the site of the friary of a religious order of friars in the 13th century called the Crutched Friars.

Pocket Fact 🌉

The fig leaf on the statue of Achilles in Park Lane was not there originally but was put there to spare the blushes of Victorian ladies.

Barge Master and Swan, Garlick Hill

This statue depicts the Barge Master and a swan. The Barge Master, in his distinctive red uniform, is in charge of the yearly marking of the monarch's swans, carried out by the Worshipful Company of Vintners, a tradition called 'swan upping'. The Vintners and the Worshipful Company of Dyers were granted rights of ownership by the Crown in the 15th century and it is their job to ring the cygnets to identify them as belonging to the Queen.

Golden Boy of Pye Corner, corner of Giltspur Street and Cock Lane

This small gold-coloured statue high up on the corner of a building commemorates where the Great Fire of London stopped. The inscription says 'This Boy is in Memmory Put up for the late FIRE of LONDON Occasion'd by the Sin of Gluttony'.

Gold statue of Justice, top of the Old Bailey Criminal Court, Newgate

The statue holds a set of scales in her left hand to balance 'truth and fairness' and the sword represents power or, as her sword is double edged, 'reason and justice'.

Pocket Fact ⫞⫞⫞

The Monument at Monument Street and Fish Hill Street was designed by Christopher Wren and was built to commemorate the Great Fire of London. The column is topped by a cauldron of flames and the base is decorated with scenes of the Great Fire. It is 202ft and if it was laid down it would reach where the fire started in Pudding Lane. It has great views over London from its viewing platform, 311 steps from the ground.

VICTORIA AND ALBERT'S STATUES

Queen Victoria ruled during the Golden Age of Britain when Britain's imperial power was at its greatest and nothing demonstrates this more than her and her husband Albert's memorial statues.

The statue of Prince Albert was commissioned by Victoria after his death in 1861. It sits opposite the Albert Hall in Kensington Gardens and the memorial is 176ft tall. A golden statue of Albert is seated under a canopy decorated with mosaics and topped with 16 statues, angels and a cross.

The memorial to Victoria outside Buckingham Palace was sculpted by Thomas Brock and completed in 1911. The surround was created by the architect Aston Webb from 2,300 tonnes of white marble. The memorial is 82ft tall with a 13ft tall statue of Victoria and is surrounded by statues representing the Victorian virtues of charity, justice, truth, motherhood and courage, and is topped by a golden winged Victory. It is affectionately known as the 'Wedding Cake'.

Pocket Tip

The steps of Queen Victoria's Memorial are an excellent place to stand to watch the Changing of the Guard (see p.55). You need to get there early – but don't climb on the statue!

3

LONDON POWERS

London is unique, as unlike many other cities its power stems not just from the national government and the monarchy but also from the financial power of the City of London. This chapter will look at the powers that rule the city, their role and how they have shaped London and its history.

🚕 THE MONARCHY 🚕

The monarchy is an integral part of London's history and its influence on London is immeasurable. Royal power infuses every part of London through palaces, parks and statues, and the monarchy continues to play an important part in the life of the city with its ceremonies and traditions. Today, the Royal Collection is responsible for the running of the royal palaces.

ROYAL ROLE IN THE CITY

The Queen still plays an important part in the life of London and people are still drawn to the capital by the pageantry, ceremony and celebration associated with the monarchy. The crowds that attend the ceremonies of Trooping the Colour, the State Opening of Parliament every year and those that attended the celebrations of the Queen's Silver Jubilee in 1977, her Golden Jubilee in 2002 and are expected to attend the Diamond Jubilee in 2012, show that the monarchy still has a place in the country.

SHAPING THE CITY: ROYAL PALACES

One of the biggest influences the monarchy has had on London is in the building of royal palaces and the creation of Westminster as the centre of government. Today the monarchy's continuing use of the royal palaces is a constant reminder of the monarch's presence and long association with London.

Whitehall Palace

Whitehall Palace was located in the area around Whitehall now used by the government and became a royal residence in 1529 when Henry VIII moved there from the Old Palace of Westminster. He spent a fortune (£11 million today) on the palace, building tennis courts, a cockfighting pit and a tiltyard (a jousting arena).

Pocket Fact

In 1542 an inventory was taken of the contents of the palace and there were over 40,000 items listed including tapestries, cloth, clothing, glassware and ceramics, maps and musical instruments.

Whitehall Palace remained in use as a palace until 1689, when King William III and Queen Mary II decided not to live there (see p.37). In 1698 a fire destroyed Whitehall Palace and only a few features remain, including the Banqueting House, the wine cellars under Whitehall and the current parade ground at Horse Guards, which was the old tiltyard of the palace.

Pocket Fact

What would Henry VIII think about Horse Guards Parade being used for the beach volleyball during the 2012 London Olympics?

St James's Palace

St James's Palace was created in the 1520s when Henry VIII decided that one palace was not enough in London. So he built a palace on the site of the former St James's leper hospital by draining the surrounding marsh land and created St James's Park for his hunting. The monarchy has continuously used St James's Palace, and today it is used for state visits by foreign representatives and receptions for charities of which the royal family are patrons. The administrative offices of princes William and Harry are based here and it is the London home of the Princess Royal and Princess Alexandra.

Some essential facts about St James's Palace:

- It is guarded by the same regiments of Footguards from the Household Division as Buckingham Palace (see p.152).

- It is the monarch's official address. All communications about the royal family are prefixed by the phrase 'St James's Palace announces . . .'

- All ambassadors and high commissioners to the UK are accredited to and received at the Court of St James.

- Princess Diana's coffin rested in the Royal Chapel before her funeral in Westminster Abbey, to allow the family to pay their respects in private.

- Every day a horse-drawn carriage delivers mail from St James's Palace to Buckingham Palace.

- Mary Tudor's heart is buried under the choir stalls in the palace and her body under her sister Queen Elizabeth I in Westminster Abbey.

- Queen Elizabeth I said her prayers in St James's Royal Chapel before the attack by the Spanish Armada in 1588.

Pocket Fact 👍

Without the royal love of hunting we would not have Hyde Park, Green Park, St James's Park, Richmond Park and Bushy Park, which were originally created as hunting grounds. For more on royal parks see p.120.

Kensington Palace

Whitehall Palace continued to be a royal residence until the reign of William III and Mary II in 1689. They found that the damp riverside location of Whitehall did not suit them because of William's asthma and so in 1689 they bought Nottingham House in Kensington. William and Mary instructed Christopher Wren to remodel the house because it was too small, but when Mary died of smallpox in 1694 the alterations were stopped and did not begin again until 1695.

Pocket Fact ⫘

Rotten Row is a broad track that runs through Hyde Park. The name comes from the French Route du Roi or King's Road, which was created by William III through Hyde Park to allow him safe passage to St James's Palace from Kensington Palace.

In 1720 King George I remodelled the palace yet again and he commissioned the beautifully decorated ceilings painted by William Kent. King George II made Kensington his main home, living there for four to six months a year until the death of his wife Queen Caroline in 1737, who did so much to the gardens we see today (see p.122). The palace fell into disrepair and was never again used as a home by a reigning monarch. Instead it became the home to the sons and relatives of the monarch.

Pocket Fact ⫘

William and Mary's move to Kensington Palace shaped the Kensington area, as wealthy people moved in and shops sprang up in the High Street and Church Street.

It was at Kensington Palace on 20 June 1837 that Princess Victoria was awakened with the news that she was now Queen of England. Victoria moved into Buckingham Palace (see p.40) and Kensington Palace again fell into disrepair until Parliament was persuaded by Victoria to pay for the renovation on the understanding that the State Apartments would be opened to the public. Today the palace is a mixture of the State Apartments, which are open to the public, and apartments for various members of the royal family including the cousins of the Queen, Prince and Princess Michael of Kent, the Duke and Duchess of Kent, and the Duke and Duchess of Gloucester. The palace's most famous resident was Princess Diana, who lived there from 1981 to 1997. Its current residents, since June 2011, are Prince William and his wife, Kate. Highlights of a visit to Kensington Palace include Queen Victoria's bedroom, the Cupola Room, the beautifully painted King's Staircase and the bed of Mary of Modena, the second wife of James II.

Pocket Tip ❙

For more details about Kensington Palace, visit the Historic Royal Palaces website (www.hrp.org.uk/KensingtonPalace/stories.aspx).

Buckingham Palace

In 1761 George III bought Buckingham House, near to St James's Palace, as a family home for his wife Queen Charlotte. It became known as the Queen's House and 14 of George III's 15 children were born there.

In 1820 George IV decided to renovate the palace as it was decided that London did not have a proper palace as befitted the capital of the greatest power in the world. In 1826 John Nash was instructed to prepare plans to renovate Buckingham Palace and Parliament was requested to provide £450,000 (£18 million today) to complete it. Although the palace building was enlarged and transformed, it is the interior of the building that was made truly awe inspiring.

Pocket Fact 🌉

George IV was known for his outlandish dress. For his first speech in the House of Lords he wore pink high heels which matched the pink satin lining of his black velvet, gold-embroidered (and pink-spangled) suit.

George IV's love of the 'flamboyant' was carried through by the designer John Nash to the decoration of the state rooms at the palace. They are staggering, with silk-covered walls, fantastic French furniture, superb works of art by masters such as Rembrandt, Canaletto and Rubens, huge chandeliers and dazzling gold leaf on the walls. Unfortunately, George did not see it finished as he died before it was completed.

Pocket Fact

Buckingham Palace was bombed nine times during the Blitz, and after the bombing the Queen said she 'could now look the East End in the face'.

Queen Victoria came to the throne in 1837 and moved into Buckingham Palace, which was finally completed in 1847. Victoria was the first sovereign to make Buckingham Palace the main residence of the monarchy in London. Victoria and Prince Albert enlarged Buckingham Palace, building an extra wing containing the Yellow Drawing Room, the Principal Corridor, the Chinese Luncheon room and the Centre Room with the famous balcony. The balcony is where the royal family have greeted thousands of well-wishers on a number of occasions, including the end of the Second World War, the marriages of Prince Charles and Princess Diana, and of Prince William and Kate Middleton, and the Queen's silver and golden jubilees.

Pocket Fact

On 8 May 1945 Buckingham Palace was the focal point for the Victory in Europe celebrations. The palace was floodlit after six years and thousands gathered on the Mall. The royal family appeared on the balcony eight times to acknowledge the cheering crowds.

Some essential facts about Buckingham Palace:

• The palace opens to the public in August and September.

- A flag always flies above Buckingham Palace. When the monarch is in residence, the Royal Standard flies and when they are not in residence, the Union Flag is flown.

- The palace has its own chapel, post office, swimming pool, staff cafeteria, doctor's surgery and cinema.

Pocket Tip 🖊

For more on Buckingham Palace, the Royal Mews or Clarence House (the home of Prince Charles), go to the Royal Collection website (www.royalcollection.org.uk).

Buckingham Palace garden parties

- *The parties were started by Queen Victoria in 1860.*
- *The names of guests are put forward by the government, armed services, charities and societies and are a way of recognising and rewarding public service.*
- *The Queen holds three garden parties at Buckingham Palace each year.*
- *The parties are attended by 10,000 people from all walks of life.*
- *Each party serves 27,000 cups of tea, 20,000 sandwiches and 20,000 slices of cake.*

FAMOUS ROYAL EVENTS WHICH HAVE TAKEN PLACE IN LONDON

- 38 coronations of the monarch have taken place in London since the first recorded coronation of William the Conqueror in 1066.

- The most lavish coronation was that of George IV in 1821 which cost £238,238 (£9 million today). The doors of Westminster Abbey were slammed in the face of George's estranged wife Caroline of Brunswick when she tried to attend the coronation.

- The processional route at the coronation of Elizabeth II on 2 June 1953 was 7.2km/4.5 miles and took the 16,000 participants two hours to complete.

- In 1953 at 9.45pm on the night of the coronation the Queen turned on 'lights of London' from the balcony at Buckingham Palace. Lights cascaded down the Mall into Trafalgar Square turning the fountains to silver until all the floodlights from the National Gallery to the Tower of London had been lit.

- In 1977, one million people lined the streets for the Queen's Silver Jubilee.

- On 6 September1997 the coffin of Princess Diana left her home, Kensington Palace, and was taken to Westminster Abbey for her funeral service. Over a million people lined the route.

- In 2002 a televised concert was held in the grounds of Buckingham Palace to celebrate the Golden Jubilee and 40,000 people watched the concert on big screens in the Mall.

- On 29 April 2011 the wedding of the Duke and Duchess of Cambridge, Prince William and Kate Middleton, took place at Westminster Abbey. An estimated one million people lined the streets to catch a glimpse of the couple – some of them sleeping out for three nights to grab the best spots.

Pocket Fact

At the wedding of the Duke and Duchess of Cambridge, an avenue of eight English native trees (two hornbeams and six field maples) lined the nave of Westminster Abbey as part of the floral decoration. The hornbeam tree signified resilience and the maple trees symbolised humility and reserve and in medieval times its wood was used to make carved loving cups.

🚕 GOVERNMENT 🚕

Westminster and Whitehall in London are the home of the British national government. In the 11th century the monarchy and the government were one, as the monarch had absolute power. In the 11th century Edward the Confessor decided to build a palace at Westminster and so it gradually became the centre of government. This palace stood for over 800 years until its destruction by fire in 1834. When the Houses of Parliament were completed in 1860 it was still called the Palace of Westminster because it had once been the site of a royal residence.

PALACE OF WESTMINSTER

In the 12th century King Henry II moved part of the treasury from its traditional home in Winchester to Westminster Palace, and in the 13th century under King John, the Exchequer, which managed and collected revenues, also moved to Westminster, meaning that all of the governing power of Britain, including the monarchy, was now based in London at the Palace of Westminster.

Pocket Fact 🌉

The Exchequer is named after the black chequered cloth with green stripes, which was used to calculate how much money was collected.

THE BEGINNING OF PARLIAMENT

Despite King John putting the Royal Seal on the Magna Carta (see p.5) in 1215, the power to govern the country was still firmly held by the monarchy, and during the reign of Henry III even the power of the barons began to lessen.

In 1258 the barons, led by Simon de Montfort, demanded that Henry III appoint a new great council of 24 men, which would include 12 barons and be elected by the barons themselves to assist the monarch in ruling the country. The King refused and Simon de Montfort led an army against him and the King was imprisoned.

Simon de Montfort summoned the Great Council and representatives from every county and larger towns.

Pocket Fact 🔔

The Great Council and the baron representatives are seen as the earliest parliament, which would later comprise the monarch, the Lords (barons) and the Commons (representatives of the counties and towns).

By the time Henry III was freed and Simon de Montfort defeated, Parliament was too well established and the risk of further uprising was too high to go back to the old ways of governing and so the new system of government remained.

The monarchy continued to live at the Palace of Westminster for the next 300 years and it was not until the 16th century when Henry VIII moved out of the Palace of Westminster that it became the permanent home of Parliament.

THE CURRENT PALACE OF WESTMINSTER

The current Palace of Westminster (or the Houses of Parliament as they are also known), was completed in 1870. The Palace has two chambers, one for the House of Lords and one for the wholly elected House of Commons. There are red seats in the House of Lords and green seats in the House of Commons.

Pocket Fact 🔔

Westminster Bridge is painted green as it is near the House of Commons, whereas Lambeth Bridge is painted red as it is near the House of Lords.

The Palace has 100 staircases, over 2 miles of corridors and over 1,100 rooms, which include offices, tea room, committee rooms, and Commons and Lords libraries, the parliamentary archives and bars.

Pocket Fact 🌉

Spencer Perceval is the only prime minister to have been assassinated. He was shot in the chest in the lobby of the House of Commons in 1812.

STRUCTURE OF THE UK GOVERNMENT

The UK government is made up of the House of Commons and the House of Lords. The House of Commons is the lower house and its members' role is to represent the interests and concerns of their constituents, consider and propose new laws, scrutinise government policies and look after the country's finances. The country is divided up into constituencies and each area has an elected Member of Parliament.

The Lords is the upper house and it plays a vital role in scrutinising legislation, proposing amendments to it and questioning the government. Generally, the decisions made in one house have to be approved by the other. In this way the two houses act as a check and balance for each other. The members of the House of Lords as of 2011 included 715 life peers appointed by the monarch on advice from the government. The non-party political life peerages are appointed by the House of Lords Appointments Commission and are either self-nominated or nominated by organisations. They are chosen on merit and the ability to make an effective contribution. There are 90 hereditary peers and when there is a vacancy a replacement is elected from all the hereditary peers in the country by the 90 in the House of Lords. 25 bishops of the Church of England are also members of this house.

Pocket Fact 🌉

As the head of the country, the monarch still gives formal approval to all laws and signs her name to every act of parliament.

THE PRIME MINISTER AND DOWNING STREET

The role of prime minister was not officially recognised until 1905 but the role began with Robert Walpole in 1720 when he was appointed First Minister by George II and subsequently given 10 Downing Street as his home in 1735. The house was built as part of a terrace of 10–15 houses in 1682 by Sir George Downing, a property speculator.

By the 1820s Downing Street had become the centre of government, and although some prime ministers preferred to remain in their own houses, in 1902 10 Downing Street became the official residence of the prime minster and every one of them since then has lived there.

Ten facts about the door at No. 10

- In 1766 Lord North added the light over the door and the lion head door knocker.

- The door has not always been black; from 1908 to 1916 it was dark green.

- When the door is painted it has five coats of paint and is sanded down between coats.

- There are two identical doors that are swapped when one needs tidying up.

- The wooden Georgian door was replaced, in 1991 by a bomb-proof metal door, but it looks like the old door.

- Despite the Georgian door being replaced, the zero is still crooked to match the original.

- The original door is in the Churchill Museum in the Churchill War Rooms.

- The brass letter box is engraved with the words 'First Lord of the Treasury'.

- The door is opened from the inside by someone watching a screen, as there is no key hole.

- 53 prime ministers have gone through the famous door.

Pocket Fact 🌉

No. 11 Downing Street is the home of the Chancellor of the Exchequer or the Second Lord of the Treasury and can be accessed from No. 10 without going outside.

WHITEHALL

The government departments are collectively known as Whitehall because they are located around the street called Whitehall. When the old Whitehall Palace burnt down in 1698 much of the land was leased for town houses. A remaining example of one of these houses is Dover House, which was built in 1755 and is now home to the Scotland Office. The other remaining houses were replaced by purpose-built offices over the years.

Government departments located in Whitehall:

- HM Revenue and Customs: the economics and finance ministry.

- Foreign and Commonwealth Office: responsible for promoting British interests overseas and supporting British citizens and businesses around the world.

- Cabinet Office: supports the prime minister and the cabinet in implementing policy and lead work to ensure the civil service provides efficient and effective support to the government.

- Wales Office: represents Wales's interests in the UK Government.

- Scotland Office: represents Scotland's interests in the UK Government.

- Ministry of Defence: is responsible for the implementation of government defence policy and is the headquarters of the British armed forces.

Pocket Fact ⚓

The Cabinet War Rooms, built underground during the Second World War, were closed in 1945, but reopened as the Churchill War Rooms in 1984. When one of the desks was being reinstalled, an officer's sugar rations were found carefully hidden in a drawer. For more details on visiting the museum visit the Churchill War Rooms website (http://cwr.iwm.org.uk).

🚌 GOVERNMENT FOR LONDON 🚌

London is the home of the national government of Britain, but it also has its own elected government; the Greater London Authority or GLA, headed by the Mayor of London.

London County Council

In 1889 the elected London County Council (LCC) was created and granted increased powers over education, city planning and council housing. The LCC also created 28 metropolitan boroughs, which covered 117 square miles and which the LCC had control over. The City of London still remained a completely separate entity though.

Several schemes were suggested and rejected for the headquarters of the LCC but eventually a site on the south side of the river near Westminster Bridge was chosen and the building of the County Hall was started in 1912.

Pocket Fact ⚓

The council discussed putting a landing strip on the roof but as aviation was a bit unknown at the time, it decided against having the strip.

Greater London Council

In 1965 London continued to expand into the surrounding boroughs, so the LCC was replaced by the Greater London

Council (GLC). The council now controlled 31 boroughs, covering 610 square miles. The council was responsible for traffic management, maintenance of main roads, refuse disposal, and the running of ambulance and fire services.

In 1986 Margaret Thatcher abolished the GLC on the grounds that it was inefficient and unnecessary and to cut bureaucracy, but there is some suggestion that it was done because the Labour party controlled the GLC and Thatcher did not think the Conservatives could gain control. The abolition left London with no strategic authority and the roles previously carried out by the GLC were now carried out by different bodies within the national government.

Pocket Fact 🌉

In 1993 a poll was taken by the London Evening Standard, *which showed that 56% of Londoners thought that the abolition of the GLC was a mistake.*

Greater London Authority

In 2000 London had its government restored with the creation of the GLA. The previous leader of the GLC Ken Livingstone was elected Mayor of London. The GLA now represents 610 square miles of the Greater London Area and shares local government powers with 33 boroughs. The GLA is responsible for transport, policing, economic development, development of strategic planning, and fire and emergency planning. It has an assembly of 25 elected members. The current mayor Boris Johnson was elected in 2008 and a mayoral election is due in 2012. The GLA headquarters, City Hall, is on the south bank of the Thames by Tower Bridge.

Pocket Fact 🌉

The GLA headquarters, designed by Norman Foster, is instantly recognisable with its bulbous shape, which has been likened to a motorcycle helmet or misshapen egg.

🚕 THE CITY OF LONDON 🚕
GOVERNMENT

The City of London Corporation is the local government responsible for the financial and commercial 'Square Mile' of the City of London. It could be compared to an independent state within London, with its own City of London police force (see p.156) and powers.

City of London coat of arms

The City of London coat of arms is a heraldic design and first appeared in the 14th century. These heraldic designs were originally worn on a tunic or shield and were unique to the person or family they represented. The City of London coat of arms is made up of a white shield with the red cross of St George, which represents England. The red sword in the left upper quarter of the shield represents St Paul, the patron saint of the City of London, and symbolises the sword that St Paul was martyred by.

The Corporation looks after the needs of around 8,000 residents and 300,000 people who come to work in the Square Mile. In addition to the normal services provided by the local authority of housing, refuse collection, education, social services, environmental health and town planning, it is also responsible for Guildhall Art Gallery, the Barbican Centre, and the Central Criminal Court at Old Bailey.

The City is responsible for a variety of organisations:

- 10,000 acres of open space including Hampstead Heath and Epping Forest.

- Three wholesale markets: Billingsgate (fish), Smithfield (meat) and New Spitalfields (fruit, vegetables and flowers).

- The Arc: Heathrow Airport's animal reception centre which catalogues every animal that comes through the airport including snow leopards, elephants, crocodiles and snakes.

The City is governed by the Court of Common Council and is divided into 25 wards, which were small medieval areas that were allowed to govern themselves. The Common Council consists of 25 aldermen, who represent the wards and who are elected every six years. The Common Council evolved from the 40 citizens that the aldermen chose from the wards in 1285 to help them administer the City. There are also 100 common councilmen, who represent the wards and are elected every four years. The aldermen and councilmen are elected by both businesses and residents. Businesses get votes according to how many people they employ.

Pocket Fact

Some of the names of the wards are named after the trades that took place there, including Candlewick, Cordwainers (shoemakers), Bread Street and Lime Street.

Some facts about the Lord Mayor

- *The Lord Mayor is elected once a year on Michaelmas (29 September) by the Common Hall made up of the liverymen of the livery companies.*
- *The post of Lord Mayor is completely separate from the GLA, and when the title Lord Mayor is used it only refers to the City of London.*
- *The Court of Common Council elect the new Lord Mayor by a show of hands and he/she takes office on the day before the Lord Mayor's show in November in the 'Silent Ceremony'.*
- *The post is unpaid and the Lord Mayor is abroad for three months of their year in office promoting the City of London.*
- *The Lord Mayor lives in the 250-year-old Georgian Mansion House opposite the Bank of England.*
- *The Lord Mayor has a working breakfast, lunch and dinner most days.*
- *The Lord Mayor makes some 900 speeches and attends 2,000 events during their year in office.*

🚕 THE CITY OF LONDON: 🚕 TRADING POWER

The City of London's motto is *Domine Dirige Nos* or 'O Lord direct (guide) us'. A more fitting motto would perhaps be 'trade, trade and more trade'. For nearly 2,000 years the City has been the financial powerhouse of the country. In the early days the City traded in goods but now it trades in finance and financial products, making it the world's richest trading city.

Pocket Fact 🌉

If the City was an independent country it would be ranked the 20th richest in the world, just ahead of Belgium!

Although not officially part of the government of London, the power and influence it has over trade makes the City one of the integral forces in London. The City knows its power, and through the ages when the monarchy needed money the City always provided financial aid in exchange for concessions and the granting of more autonomy. This attitude has prevailed within the City and has led it to being constantly at odds with Westminster, whether the monarchy or the government. The livery companies or trade guilds have always been heavily involved in governing the City and this has ensured that any political decisions they are involved in promoted trade.

FROM TRADE TO FINANCE: TIMELINE OF THE CITY

7th century

- Lundenwic is founded to the west of the City by the Anglo-Saxons and described by Bede as 'the mart (market) of many nations resorting to it by land and sea'.
- During this time the guilds (trade organisations) begin.

11th century

- Denmark's King Cnut stabilises English coinage, leading to increased foreign trade.

16th century

- Thomas Gresham, member of the Mercers Guild, establishes the Royal Exchange at Threadneedle Street where sellers met buyers, and also the first private bank.

Pocket Fact

London's merchants wanted an exchange like Venice and Antwerp to trade commodities so a site was found in Cornhill to build the London Exchange. It was given the 'Royal' title by Elizabeth I in 1571.

17th century

- The Bank of England is founded as the central bank for the UK. Originally privately owned, it is now owned by HM Revenue and Customs and is responsible for issuing notes and setting interest rates.

- Stock dealers are expelled from the Royal Exchange for being too rowdy and start to meet in coffee houses.

- Richard Hoare establishes his bank as one of the first private deposit banks in Cheapside.

Pocket Fact

Messrs Hoare Bank still exists in Fleet Street and is still run by the descendants of the founder Richard Hoare. Alexander Hoare is the 11th-generation chief executive.

18th century

- The Bank of England moves to new premises in Threadneedle Street.

- Barings Bank, the first merchant bank, is founded.

- Daily cheque clearings begin when the bank clerks meet at the Five Bells, a tavern in Lombard Street, to exchange all their cheques in one place and settle the balances in cash.

19th century

- 11 new merchant banks, including the Rothschild, are founded following the removal of restrictive legislation.

- In 1897 Britain is described as the general bank for the whole world.

20th century

- The stock exchange is deregulated and the City increases its global financial reputation. Deregulation allows the banks such as Barclays, Citigroup and HSBC to buy out the old stock-broking companies and trade on the stock exchange.

21ST CENTURY: THE CURRENT STATE OF CITY TRADE

- There is £1.9 trillion of foreign exchange turnover per day, 37% of the global market.

- It forms 70% of the global Euro bond market.

- There are 249 international banks in the City.

- There are 551 companies listed on the London Stock Exchange.

- Around 300,000 people work in the City.

🚕 POMP AND CIRCUMSTANCE 🚕

There is probably no other city in the world that has as many ceremonies and processions throughout the year as London. They are full of tradition and colour and these are the ones not to be missed.

CHANGING OF THE GUARD

Location: Buckingham Palace

When: At 11.15am every day from May to July (alternate days from August to April). During very wet weather no change takes place.

What happens: Buckingham Palace is guarded by the Queen's Guard and St James's Palace by the St James's Palace Detachment. When guardsmen are on duty the guard will be from one of the five regiments of the Footguards: the Grenadier, Coldstream, Scots, Irish and Welsh Guards, who wear the traditional red tunics and bearskin hats (see p.152). During the Changing of the Guard the new guards march into the palace accompanied by the guard's band and the ceremony of the new guard exchanging duty with the old guard takes place, while a variety of music is played. The old guard then marches out.

CHANGING OF THE HOUSEHOLD CAVALRY

Location: Horse Guards, Whitehall

When: 11am on weekdays, 10am on Sundays

What happens: Every day the Household Cavalry, which is made up of the Life Guards and the Blues and Royals, rides down from the Hyde Park Barracks at Knightsbridge to take over guard duties at Horse Guards Parade. The mounted regiments consist of either the 'Long Guard' if the Queen is in residence, consisting of one officer, two non-commissioned officers and 10 troopers, or the 'Short Guard' if she is away and then there is no officer in attendance.

STATE OPENING OF PARLIAMENT

Location: Houses of Parliament

When: In October, November or December each year, but sometimes in a different month if a general election has taken place.

What happens: Before the Queen goes to Parliament, the Queen's Body Guard of the Yeomen of the Guard searches the cellars of the Houses of Parliament, a tradition which dates back to 1605 and the Gunpowder Plot (see p.9). A 'hostage' Member of Parliament (generally the parliamentary secretary to the Treasury) is also held at Buckingham Palace to ensure the safe return of the monarch.

The Queen travels from Buckingham Palace to Parliament accompanied by the Imperial State Crown in its own carriage. The carriage is escorted by the Household Cavalry and the route is guarded by the Guards. Inside, Black Rod (a senior officer in the House of Lords), acting as the Queen's messenger, tries to deliver the message which summons members of the House of Commons to the House of Lords to hear the Queen's Speech, which sets out her government's legislative programme for the year ahead. As he/she tries to enter, the door of the Commons is slammed in his/her face as no monarch has set foot in the House of Commons since Charles I tried to arrest five Members of Parliament in 1642.

Pocket Tip 🖋
You can view the procession to Parliament from Buckingham Palace from the Mall and Whitehall.

TROOPING THE COLOUR

Location: Horse Guards Parade, Whitehall

When: June

What happens: The monarch's birthday is officially celebrated by the ceremony of Trooping the Colour on a Saturday in June. The Queen and other members of the royal family and invited guests take the salute of 1,400 officers and men on parade from the five Footguards regiments, 200 horses from the Household Cavalry and Royal Horse Artillery and 400 musicians from 10 bands. The Queen then returns to the palace accompanied by her guards. She then joins other members of the royal family on the palace balcony to watch the flypast by the Royal Air Force.

Pocket Tip ❚
You can view the procession to and from Buckingham Palace or apply for tickets in the seated stands for the rehearsals at Horse Guards Parade the week before.

LORD MAYOR'S SHOW

Location: The procession leaves Mansion House for the Royal Courts of Justice in the Strand at 11am. It returns from Victoria Embankment to Mansion House at 1pm.

When: November

What happens: The new Lord Mayor travels in the gold Lord Mayor's coach to the Royal Courts of Justice to swear allegiance to the Crown. The procession is spectacular and stretches for 3 miles. It includes bands, decorated floats, impressive wicker-giants Gog and Magog (the traditional guardians of the City of London) and many horse-drawn carriages. The day finishes at 5pm with a huge firework display. It is best to get there early and the best view is from Victoria Embankment.

Pocket Fact ⚓
Gog and Magog are mythical giants and were said to be the founders and guardians of the City of London. They were first carried in the Lord Mayor's procession in the 15th century.

FREEDOMS OF THE CITY OF LONDON

Location: The Guildhall

When: If your application is successful or an honorary Freedom is being given.

What happens: The first Freedom was awarded in 1237. To apply to be a freeman you can do any of the following:

- Serve an apprenticeship to a freeman.

- Be the child of a freeman.

- Be a member of one of the City livery companies.

- Apply for the Freedom by nomination. You must be nominated by two sponsors who will be common councilmen of the City of London, aldermen or members of a livery company.

- You can also be made a freeman without the need for application by being on the electoral role for over one year. Applicants need to advise the Chamberlain's Court that they are on the Ward List.

The prospective freeman reads the 'Declaration of a Freeman', which includes swearing allegiance to the sovereign and obedience to the Lord Mayor. Around 2,000 people are granted the Freedom of the City per year.

Some Freedoms of the City

- *The right to earn money and own land.*
- *The right to herd sheep over London Bridge (although some argue that the right was actually not to have to pay the toll to do so).*
- *The right to go about the City with a drawn sword.*
- *If convicted of a capital offence the right to be hanged with a silken rope.*
- *The right to be drunk and disorderly without fear of arrest.*

The highest honour is not to apply to be a freeman but to be invited by the Common Council to take the Freedom. The ceremony takes place before the Lord Mayor, aldermen, common councilmen and invited guests, and is followed by a banquet.

Seven famous honorary freemen

- *The Queen*
- *Princess Diana*
- *Nelson Mandela*
- *Florence Nightingale*
- *General Eisenhower*
- *Theodore Roosevelt*
- *Winston Churchill*

4

LITERARY LONDON

From Charles Dickens's descriptions of a foggy, poverty ridden Victorian London to Monica Ali and the pressures of living in the Bangladesh community of Brick Lane, London provides a wealth of material for writers. Many famous authors were born in London, such as Geoffrey Chaucer, John Milton, Virginia Woolf and Nick Hornby, while others such as George Orwell and Oscar Wilde were inspired by the time they spent living in the city.

This chapter will provide key information about some of the authors who were born in London and those who have featured it in their work, while describing some of London's literary 'hot spots'. You will also find some suggestions for the best bookshops and book buying areas around London.

🚗 LITERARY FIGURES 🚗
FROM LONDON

From the 14th century to the present day London has continued to produce famous authors. Here are just a few of London's most famous literary offspring.

GEOFFREY CHAUCER

Chaucer's actual date and place of birth are unknown but are thought to be around 1343 and assumed to be in London, as his father was a London vintner (wine merchant). Chaucer was very well educated and was a philosopher, alchemist and astronomer, and had an active career in the civil service as a diplomat. Chaucer is considered to be the father of English literature as he wrote in the English vernacular language at a time when French and Latin were the dominant languages for the educated classes and for any respected literary works.

Pocket Fact ◢━━◣

Wynkyn de Worde from Alsace was assistant to William Caxton (the first English printer). After Caxton's death in 1491, de Worde moved the business to Fleet Street, thereby starting its long association with printing, which continued until the 1980s. De Worde was the first printer to print relatively inexpensive books such as Lives of the Saints *and* The Canterbury Tales *for a commercial audience.*

Chaucer's most famous work is *The Canterbury Tales*, a set of poems written about a story-telling contest between pilgrims travelling from Southwark in London to the shrine of St Thomas Becket in Canterbury. The tales are a commentary on medieval life with characters such as the miller, nuns and priests, and the knight each telling their stories. Chaucer lived in London nearly all his life and is buried in Poets' Corner in Westminster Abbey. It is said that it was his burial in that corner of the church that started its long association with writers.

Pocket Fact ◢━━◣

Poet's Corner in Westminster Abbey contains the graves of many famous authors including Rudyard Kipling, Thomas Hardy and Alfred Tennyson, and memorials to the Brontë sisters, Robert Burns and Lewis Carroll.

JOHN MILTON

Milton was born in Bread Street in 1608 and came from a wealthy family. He was very well educated at St Paul's School in London and Cambridge University, where he started to write poetry in Latin. During the English Civil War in the 1640s he was on the side of Oliver Cromwell and published several pamphlets attacking the Anglican Church. In 1660 when the monarchy was restored, Milton went into hiding fearing for his life and his writings were burnt instead. In 1651 he went totally blind, and it was during this time in 1667 that he wrote his most famous poem *Paradise Lost* about the Fall of Man and the temptation of Adam and Eve. He died in 1674.

London Literary Hot Spot 🚌

John Milton is buried in St Giles' without Cripplegate church, St Giles Terrace.

SAMUEL PEPYS

Pepys was a famous diarist born near Fleet Street in London in 1633 and was educated in St Paul's School and Cambridge University. He began his diaries on 1 January 1660, writing in a form of shorthand. The observations in his diaries give us huge insight into what were very turbulent times for London, including the coronation of Charles II in 1660, the plague of 1665 and the Great Fire of London in 1666.

Pocket Fact 🌉

Pepys describes London burning during the Great Fire with great emotion: 'We staid till, it being darkish, we saw the fire as only one entire arch of fire from this to the other side of the bridge, and in a bow up the hill for an arch of above a mile long: it made me weep to see it.'

Pepys stopped writing his diary in 1669 as he was afraid that the writing was too hard on his eyes and he might go blind, although this fear was unfounded as he retained his sight until his death in 1703. Pepys is buried in St Olave's, Hart Street.

Other famous 16th- and 17th-century writers born in London

John Donne: Donne was born in 1572 in Bread Street and was a priest, poet, satirist and lawyer and a contemporary of Shakespeare. He is famous for his sermons, sonnets, elegies, pamphlets and poems such as *The Good-Morrow* and *Woman's Constancy*. Donne penned the well-known phrase 'No man is an island'.

Daniel Defoe: Defoe was born in 1660 in the area of St Giles, Cripplegate. He wrote more than 500 books and pamphlets as a businessman, journalist, pamphleteer and prolific author. His works include *Robinson Crusoe* (1719), the story of a shipwrecked man, and *Moll Flanders* (1722), which is set in London.

Pocket Tip

For a wide selection of specialist, second-hand and antiquarian bookshops go to Charing Cross Road between Leicester Square and Cambridge Circus. Make sure you go down the little pedestrianised alleys such as Cecil Court.

WILLIAM BLAKE

Blake was born in Broadwick Street in Soho in 1757 and was a painter, poet and printmaker, who became very influential in the poetry and art of the English Romantic movement. In 1794 Blake wrote a very moving poem called *London* about the misery he found while walking on the streets of London:

> *'I wander thro' each charter'd street,*
> *Near where the charter'd Thames does flow,*
> *And mark in every face I meet*
> *Marks of weakness, marks of woe.'*

Blake died penniless and unknown in 1827 but his poems and accompanying illustrations have gone on to be highly influential in English poetry.

London Literary Hot Spot

William Blake is buried in Bunhill Fields, City Road, where his fans leave offerings of coins, perhaps because he died a pauper and spent his last money on pencils so that he could finish his sketches for Dante's Inferno.

JOHN KEATS

Keats was one of the principal poets of the English Romantic movement, producing literature which focused on emotion, passion, and the natural world. He was born in 1795 and died of tuberculosis aged just 25 in Rome in 1821.

Pocket Fact

John Keats was the son of Thomas Keats, a stable hand at the Swan and Hoop Inn. The Inn is now the 'The Keats at the Globe' pub in Moorgate.

During Keats's short life his poetry was not well received, but by the end of the 19th century he had become one of England's most popular poets and provided inspiration to 20th-century poets such as Wilfred Owen, W. B. Yeats and T. S. Eliot. Keats left us with wonderful poetry such as *Ode on a Grecian Urn*, *Ode to a Nightingale* and *To Autumn*.

London Literary Hot Spot

Keats House in Hampstead, where Keats wrote Ode to a Nightingale *and where he met the 'girl next door' Fanny Brawne, is now a museum. For more details, visit the Keats website (www.keatshouse.cityoflondon.gov.uk).*

MARY SHELLEY

Mary Shelley was the daughter of the famous philosopher, educator and writer Mary Wollstonecraft, the author of *The Rights of Women*, and William Godwin who was a journalist, philosopher and novelist. Mary never knew her mother – she died 10 days after Mary was born in 1797 in Somers Town. Mary was destined to be a writer not only because of her parentage but because she grew up surrounded by the friends of her father, who included Charles Lamb, Samuel Taylor Coleridge, and Percy Bysshe Shelley, with whom she eloped at the age of 17. Mary was a prolific writer of a number of novels, her most famous being *Frankenstein*, which was published anonymously when she was just 20.

London Literary Hot Spot 🚌

Mary Shelley's father, William Godwin owned a bookshop at 41 Skinner Street, where Mary met Percy Bysshe Shelley. Mary was living at 24 Chester Square when she died in 1851.

London's best big bookshops

- **Foyles, Charing Cross Road**. *This stocks Britain's widest selection of books plus year-round literary and music events.*
- **Waterstone's, Piccadilly**. *This has seven floors of books.*
- **Hatchards, Piccadilly**. *This is the oldest surviving bookshop in London (opened in 1797).*
- **Stanfords, Long Acre**. *This was established in 1853 and is considered to be the biggest travel bookshop in the world. It also has an excellent café.*

ANTHONY TROLLOPE

Anthony Trollope was a prolific writer in the 19th century, who managed to top the bestsellers list during the mid-Victorian period while still holding a full-time job with the Post Office until 1867. He was born in 1815 at Keppel Street and is most famous for his series the *Chronicles of Barsetshire*.

Pocket Fact 🌉

Trollope used several London locations in his novels. Belgrave Square is the location for the town house of Lord Grex in The Duke's Children *and several of his characters in* The Prime Minister *have homes in Berkeley Square.*

Trollope became the most published author of the time, writing several novels set in London including the series *The Pallisers*, *The Claverings* and *Sir Harry Hotspur of Humblethwaite*. He continued to write until his death in 1882 and is buried in Kensal Green Cemetery.

London's specialist bookshops

- **The Travel Bookshop, 13–15 Blenheim Crescent:** *stocks literature and guidebooks on every single country on the planet and was the inspiration for the bookshop in the film* Notting Hill.
- **Daunt Books, Marylebone High Street:** *Edwardian bookshop with long oak galleries where the books are arranged by country so guides, maps, non-fiction and fiction all sit side by side.*
- **Blackwells, Charing Cross Road:** *stocks a wide range of academic books on a multitude of subjects.*
- **Bernard J. Shapero Rare Books, 32 St George Street:** *London's leading antiquarian bookseller specialising in rare and first edition books on history, travel and English literature.*
- **Persephone Books, Lamb's Conduit Street:** *Bookshop and publisher of mainly women's fiction published during the inter-war years which are out of print by authors such as Katherine Mansfield, Virginia Woolf and Frances Hodgson Burnett.*

Other famous 18th- and 19th-century writers born in London

Robert Browning: Robert Browning was born in 1812 in Camberwell and was known for his dramatic verse and narrative poems such as *The Pied Piper of Hamelin* and *The Ring and the Book*. Browning is probably just as famous for his relationship with Elizabeth Barrett, born in 1806 in County Durham. They began a long correspondence and their courtship was conducted in secret.

In 1846 they eloped and married at St Marylebone parish church. They left immediately for Italy where Elizabeth was to die in Robert's arms in 1861 (he died in 1889). Her *Sonnets from the Portuguese* published in 1850, contain the romantic lines, 'How do I love thee? Let me count the ways'.

Edward Lear: Lear was born in Holloway in 1812 and he was an artist, illustrator, author and poet. He is particularly known for his nonsense poems especially his limericks. His most famous work is the *Owl and the Pussycat*.

VIRGINIA WOOLF

Virginia Woolf was a novelist, essayist, biographer and critic. She was born at Hyde Park Gate in 1882 and was part of an intellectual group of authors, artists, art critics and economists known as the Bloomsbury Group. These individuals were renowned for their somewhat eccentric lifestyle, and despite being married to Leonard Woolf, Virginia had a number of relationships with women, including Vita Sackville West, the author and poet. Virginia began writing professionally in 1900 for *The Times Literary Supplement* and published her first novel *The Voyage Out* in 1915.

The Bloomsbury Group

The Bloomsbury Group consisted of a group of like-minded friends who had first met at Cambridge University and then went on to meet regularly in the early 1900s at the home of Thorby Stephen at 46 Gordon Square in Bloomsbury. When Thorby died of typhoid in 1906, the meetings then took place at the homes of Vanessa Bell, the artist, and Adrian Stephen, a psychoanalyst (the sister and brother of Virginia Woolf), and also at the home of Virginia and her husband Leonard Woolf at 52 Tavistock Square.

> *The group, which included Duncan Grant, Clive Bell, John Maynard Keynes, Roger Fry and the critic and biographer Lytton Strachey, met informally to discuss art, literature and philosophy. It was hugely influential in these areas and promoted new attitudes to feminism, pacifism and sexuality.*

Virginia and Leonard Woolf founded the Hogarth Press in 1917, which published Virginia's own novels as well as works by E. M. Forster, John Maynard Keynes, T. S. Eliot and Edith Sitwell.

London Literary Hot Spot 🚌

Virginia Woolf lived at 17 The Green, and Hogarth House, Paradise Road in Richmond. Hogarth Press was named after her home.

Woolf's most successful novels were *Mrs Dalloway*, *To the Lighthouse*, *Orlando* and *The Waves*. *Mrs Dalloway* contains some excellent descriptions of post-war London in the 1920s as Clarissa Dalloway travels around London preparing for her party in the evening. Virginia Woolf suffered several bouts of depression and breakdowns, and in 1941 she committed suicide by drowning in the River Ouse near her home in Sussex.

Pocket Tip 🕯

Join in guided walks in the Bloomsbury area to trace not just its literary past but the history of the architecture and the building of the squares. For more details, visit the London Walks and blue badge guide websites (www.walks.com or www. blue-badge-guides.com).

JOHN BETJEMAN

John Betjeman was born in Highgate in 1906 and was a prolific writer publishing many works of poems. He is most famous for his poetry and published his first book of poems, *Mount Zion*, in 1931. He also wrote as a film critic for the *Evening Standard*, produced a series of Shell Guides to the counties of England and was an assistant editor of the *Architectural Review*.

Pocket Fact ⚓

There is a wonderful statue of Betjeman in St Pancras Station, which he saved from demolition in the 1960s. The sculptor Martin Jennings captured the poet's dishevelled appearance, with knotted string for one shoelace and a misshapen suit. The poet is shown looking up at the magnificent ceiling of the station he loved so much.

Betjeman's poetry was extremely popular as it was easy to read and appealed to a wide number of people. In the 1950s he became even better known from his radio and television appearances, commenting on architecture and campaigning for threatened buildings. Betjeman's works of *Collected Poems* and *Summoned by Bells* were bestsellers and he made two documentaries, *Metroland* and *A Passion for Churches*. John Betjeman died in 1984.

London Literary Hot Spot 🚌

Sylvia Plath and Ted Hughes were married at the church of St George the Martyr in Holborn.

PETER ACKROYD

Peter Ackroyd is a novelist, biographer and poet and is famous for writing about London. He was born in West Acton in 1954 and began his career as a literary editor of the *Spectator* magazine in 1973. Many of Ackroyd's books revolve around London, where he interweaves historical events with a modern-day narrative. He has published a number of novels using this method including *The Great Fire of London*, *Hawksmoor* and *The House of Doctor Dee*. Peter Ackroyd's most famous book about London is *London: A Biography*.

Other famous 20th-century writers born in London

E. M. Forster: Born in Dorset Square, Forster was a novelist, short story writer, essayist and librettist. His travels through India and Egypt provided material for his best-known novels *A Passage to India*, *A Room with a View* and *Howards End*, which were adapted for film.

Ruth Rendell: Rendell was born in South Woodford. She writes psychological thrillers and murder mysteries and also writes under the pseudonym of Barbara Vine. Her most famous novels are the 'Inspector Wexford' series, which was also adapted for television.

London Literary Hot Spot 🚌

Albany, Piccadilly, was the home to Graham Greene, Aldous Huxley, Lord Byron and J. B. Priestley.

🚗 LITERARY FIGURES WHO HAVE 🚗 LIVED IN LONDON

There are so many writers who have come to live in London and to be inspired by living and working in the city. Many of these authors have become so synonymous with their adopted city that it is surprising to find that they were not born in London, for example the great Charles Dickens.

WILLIAM SHAKESPEARE

William Shakespeare was born in 1564 in Stratford-upon-Avon. He is without doubt the most famous playwright in the world and it is a testament to his skills that his plays are still being performed over 400 years after they were written. Shakespeare appears in London in 1592 as an actor and playwright. It is unsure whether he had been in London before this as there is no record of his whereabouts from 1585 to 1592. Shakespeare's acting career started with the Lord Chamberlain's company, which was renamed the King's Company in 1603. It was in this company that Shakespeare met Richard Burbage, with whom he formed a partnership that owned interests in the Globe (see p.93) and Blackfriars theatres.

SAMUEL JOHNSON

Samuel Johnson or Dr Johnson's most famous work was *A Dictionary of the English Language* published in 1755. Johnson was born in Lichfield in Staffordshire in 1709 and became known as a writer, critic, political essayist and journalist. Although best known for his dictionary he also wrote a number of works including *Rasselas* and a description of his travels with his biographer, James Boswell, *A Journey to the Western Islands of Scotland*. Johnson lived just off Fleet Street in Gough Square, where, with the help of six assistants, he published his famous dictionary after eight years of work.

Although Johnson's dictionary was not the first, it was the most widely used for 150 years until the publication of the *Oxford English Dictionary*. James Boswell's biography of Dr Johnson, *A Life of Johnson*, was published in 1791and made Johnson famous, perhaps even more so than his own work had done. Johnson died in 1784 and is buried in Westminster Abbey.

Other famous literary figures who lived in London in the 16th, 17th and 18th centuries

Christopher Marlowe: Marlowe was an Elizabethan poet and playwright and his work included *The Jew of Malta*, *The Tragical History of Doctor Faustus* and *Hero and Leander*. Over the years there has been some controversy over the authorship of Shakespeare's plays and there are some who say that it was actually Marlowe who wrote the plays. He was killed in a tavern in Deptford in 1593 after getting into a drunken fight but some say that he did not die but was spirited away as he was a spy for Elizabeth I's spymaster Walsingham.

Jane Austen: Jane Austen stayed at the home of her brother Henry Austen when visiting her publisher in London. In 1813 just after *Pride and Prejudice* was published, Austen visited 10 Henrietta Street to nurse Henry's dying wife Eliza and visited again when *Mansfield Park* was published in 1814. Jane visited 23 Hans Place twice in 1814 and then from October to December in 1815 when Henry was ill.

CHARLES DICKENS

No discussion on London's literature would be complete without Charles Dickens. His stories capture London during the Victorian era with the vivid descriptions of London life and its people. Novels such as *Bleak House*, *Oliver Twist* and *Little Dorrit* reflect the huge gulf between rich and poor, and the hopelessness and poverty of some people, in the 19th century.

Dickens's descriptions of Victorian London are excellent and in this quote from *Oliver Twist* you can almost smell the meat market at Smithfield:

> *'It was market-morning. The ground was covered, nearly ankle-deep, with filth and mire; a thick steam, perpetually rising from the reeking bodies of the cattle, and mingling with the fog, which seemed to rest upon the chimney-tops, hung heavily above.'*

Dickens was born in Portsmouth in 1812 in a well-off family but when Dickens was nine, his father was imprisoned in the Marshalsea prison in London (later to appear in *Little Dorrit*) for bad debt. Dickens was sent to work in Warrens Blacking Factory at the age of 12. He was never to forget this experience of poverty, child labour and dirt and it informed his writing. Eventually his family circumstances improved after the death of his grandmother.

Pocket Fact 🌉

The man who taught Dickens to paste labels on the blacking pots at the factory at Hungerford Stairs (on the Thames near the Strand) was called Bob Fagin. Dickens often used people he had met and their names in his books.

Dickens began his career as a journalist and became very familiar with London as he walked around the streets on assignments. His first novel, *Pickwick Papers*, was published in 1836 in instalments, as it was too expensive for most people to purchase a whole book. Dickens was an instant success and published over 12 novels, a number of short story collections, poetry, plays and non-fiction and also found the time to edit weekly periodicals. Dickens died in 1870 and is buried in Westminster Abbey in Poets' Corner.

Pocket Tip ✒

The Dickens Museum is at 48 Doughty Street and contains paintings, rare editions, manuscripts, original furniture and other items relating to the life and work of Dickens. For more details, go to the museum's website (www.dickensmuseum.com).

Other famous literary figures who lived in London in the 19th century

George Eliot: Eliot was the pen name of Mary Ann Evans. She published under a man's name so that her work would be taken seriously at a time when women mainly penned light romances.

Eliot was a novelist and journalist and a leading writer of the 19th century. Her novels include *Middlemarch*, *Mill on the Floss*, *Silas Marner* and *Daniel Deronda*.

Henry James: James was an American who took British citizenship in 1916. He was a prolific writer, publishing 20 novels, 112 stories and 12 plays. James's most famous novels include *The Portrait of a Lady*, *The Bostonians*, *A London Life* and *The Ambassadors*.

GEORGE ORWELL

George Orwell's real name was Eric Arthur Blair. He was a journalist and author of two of the most famous novels in the 20th century: *1984* and *Animal Farm*. In 1927 Orwell lived in the Portobello Road after resigning from the Indian Imperial Police. He used many of his experiences in London for his writings, including the tradition of poor Londoners spending the summer hop picking in Kent. It was in London that he met a man who took him back to a doss house in Tooley Street where Orwell dressed and lived as a tramp and subsequently wrote about this in *Down and Out in Paris and London* in 1933.

Orwell lived in several locations in London including Uxbridge, Hampstead, Kentish Town, Greenwich and Kilburn. He was living in Islington when *Animal Farm* was published in 1945. Orwell died in 1950.

London Literary Hot Spot
The pubs The Marquis of Granby, 2 Rathbone Street, and the Fitzroy Tavern, Charlotte Street, were meeting places for George Orwell, Dylan Thomas and Augustus John and T. S. Eliot.

NICK HORNBY

Nick Hornby is a journalist, author and screenwriter. He was born in 1957 in Redhill in Surrey and lives in Highbury, North London. His first book *Fever Pitch* was published in 1992 and is an autobiographical account about his fanatical support for Arsenal football club. It was later adapted as a play and film starring Colin Firth. Many of Hornby's novels are set in London including his first novel *High Fidelity* (1995) about a record shop owner in Islington (also made into a film but set in Chicago) and *About a Boy* (1998), made into a film starring Hugh Grant. Hornby's subsequent novels *How to be Good* (2001), *Speaking with the Angel* (2001), *A Long Way Down* (2005) and *Slam* (2005) are all set in London.

Other famous literary figures living in London in the 20th and 21st century

Monica Ali: Ali was born in 1967 of English and Bangladeshi parents and lives in South London. Her first novel *Brick Lane* (2003) tells the story of an immigrant woman Nazneen who lives in the Bangladeshi community around Brick Lane in East London. Her third novel *In the Kitchen* (2009) is set in the Imperial Hotel in Piccadilly and charts the lives of the large immigrant community living and working in London.

Helen Fielding: Fielding was born in West Yorkshire in 1958 and lives in London. Her newspaper columns, the novels and subsequent film adaptations of *Bridget Jones' Diary* (1996) and *Bridget Jones: The Edge of Reason* (1999) chronicle the life of a thirty-something woman living in London.

🚕 TOP TEN BOOKS SET 🚕 IN LONDON

- *Sherlock Holmes* stories by Sir Arthur Conan Doyle are set in Victorian London.

- *The Buddha of Suburbia* (1987) by Hanif Kureishi tells the story of young Pakistani growing up in the 1970s in South London.

- *Under the Net* (1954) by Iris Murdoch is the story of a struggling young writer set in 1950s London.

- The Gemma James and Duncan Kincaid mysteries by Deborah Crombie. These are murder mysteries about two Scotland Yard detectives and are set in various locations in London. Crombie's latest novel is *Necessary as Blood* and is set in London's East End.

- *The End of the Affair* (1951) by Graham Greene. Set in London after the Second World War, it is the story of love, obsession and jealousy between three central characters.

- *Love in a Cold Climate* (1949) by Nancy Mitford is set between the two world wars and is about an aristocratic family in the privileged world of the country house and London society.

- *Saturday* (2005) by Ian McEwan set in London in 2003 it tells the story of a neurosurgeon who is having a family meal on the day a large demonstration is taking place against the Iraq war.

- *Dark Fire* (2004) by C. J. Sansom is set in Tudor London and is one of a series of stories about the lawyer Matthew Shardlake.

- *A Week in December* (2009) by Sebastian Faulks is a modern contemporary novel set in December 2007 about a dinner party attended by people from a variety of London backgrounds including a barrister, hedge fund owner and Islamic manufacturer.

- *Stoneheart* (2006) by Charlie Fletcher is a wonderful children's book set in an alternative London where the statues in London come to life after George Chapman accidentally damages one of the sculptures outside the Natural History Museum.

Pocket Tip

London's Literary Festival is an annual event at the South Bank Centre in June/July and offers contemporary writing in fiction, poetry, politics and art. There are readings by a wide range of authors and staged adaptations. See www.literaryfestivals.co.uk for more details.

5

CULTURAL LONDON

London is one of the most vibrant and diverse cultural cities in the world. With its museums, art galleries, theatres, and music venues it is said that you could do something different every day of the year. This chapter will guide you through those must-see and slightly quirkier aspects of London's culture.

🚕 MUSEUMS 🚕

In the 18th and 19th centuries there was a burst of cultural activity in the city and four of the most famous museums in London were founded, making London the home of some of the most treasured artefacts in the world, and the place to find some of the most famous and varied museums in the world.

THE BRITISH MUSEUM

The British Museum can claim to be the earliest museum of world art and artefacts in the world. In the 18th century people began to take a different intellectual approach to the study of the world, and started to observe and investigate the human and the natural world rather than just accept established theories. There was a desire to travel and to collect and study objects from many different cultures including Rome and Greece.

Hans Sloane

The physician Sir Hans Sloane (1660–1753) had always had a fascination with observing plants and animals and he embraced the investigatory spirit of the age, beginning his own collection of plant and animal specimens. In 1687 he accompanied the Duke of Albemarle to Jamaica, where he collected 800 species of plants and other live specimens.

Pocket Fact

Hans Sloane drank chocolate mixed with water in Jamaica and believed in its health-giving properties. To make it more palatable he mixed it with milk. This recipe was later purchased by Messrs Cadbury and commercially produced.

By the time of his death at the age of 93, Sloane's collection comprised 71,000 objects and he bequeathed the collection to the nation on payment of £20,000 to his heirs. This collection formed the beginning of the British Museum.

Pocket Fact

Sloane's collection was visited by the great and the good. When the composer Handel visited he annoyed his host by placing a hot buttered muffin on one of his rare books.

By the end of the 18th century the collection had outgrown its first home in Montagu House as more and more people donated their collections, including the collection of Sir William Hamilton, the ambassador to Naples. Hamilton collected antiquities from Roman towns and villas buried by the eruption of Vesuvius in AD 79, as well as painted Greek vases. These additions changed the emphasis of the museum from being primarily about books, manuscripts and natural history to art and antiquity.

The museum was bursting at the seams when the purchase of the Parthenon Sculptures from Lord Elgin put even more pressure on the museum's limited space. In 1823 Robert Smirke presented a plan to the trustees to pull down the old building and replace it with a larger new building.

Pocket Fact ◢══╲

The expeditions by Captain Cook resulted in even more objects being added to the collection, including the remains of the first kangaroo ever seen in Europe.

The new building

The planned internal courtyard was to have a garden but the British Museum Library, which has a copy of every book published, was running out of space so the garden was replaced by the Round Reading Room designed by Sydney Smirke.

As museum visitor numbers increased, it became very difficult to negotiate around all the bookshelves to find the galleries, so in 1974 it was decided to move the British Library to a new home at St Pancras. Beginning in 1998, after the collection of books was moved to the new British Library, the circular British Library Reading Room was restored and the largest enclosed space in Europe, 'The Great Court' designed by Norman Foster, was built.

Pocket Fact ◢══╲

The British Library Reading Room has been used by many famous people such as Karl Marx, Lenin, Oscar Wilde, George Bernard Shaw and Charles Dickens.

Highlights of the British Museum

- **Enlightenment**. This has 18th-century and the early collections including the oldest object in the museum, the Olduvai stone chopping tool, which is 1.8 to 2 million years old.

- **Ancient near East**. The Assyrian winged bull is the heaviest item in the museum.

- **Asia**. This contains one of the finest collections of Japanese and Chinese decorative arts, including Japanese Kakiemon elephants and Chinese ceramic tomb figures.

- **Britain and Europe**. This contains Iron Age and Roman objects including the Sutton Hoo Ship Burial and Lewis Chessmen.

- **Egypt and the Sudan**. Includes the Rosetta Stone and the Egyptian mummies from 3300 BC.

- **Greece and Rome**. This has the Parthenon Sculptures.

Pocket Tip 🖋

Go to the British Museum website (www.britishmuseum.org) for details of tours, current exhibitions and late night opening details.

PRINCE ALBERT'S MUSEUMS

In 1851 Prince Albert, husband to Queen Victoria, realised his idea to hold a great exhibition to showcase Britain as an industrial world leader. The exhibition was held in the huge Crystal Palace that was specially built in Hyde Park. It was predicted to be a disaster but six million people visited it and with the profits Prince Albert bought an area of Kensington to build museums. These museums were the Victoria and Albert Museum (V&A), the Natural History Museum and the Science Museum.

Pocket Fact 🌉

The Kensington museum area is also known as 'Albertropolis'.

Natural History Museum

This museum was opened in 1881 and contains the collection of natural curiosities that were previously housed in the British Museum. Alfred Waterhouse designed the museum in a Romanesque style and this design is as much of a curiosity as the museum itself. Built from buff and cobalt-blue terracotta tiles, it is richly decorated on both its inside and outside with elaborate sculptures of plants and animals.

The collection is vast and covers almost all groups of animals, plants, minerals and fossils, including specimens of the dodo to a full-size blue whale skeleton. In 1985 it was decided to merge the museum with the Geological Museum, which has an amazing collection of rocks, minerals and fossils.

Five wonders of the Natural History Museum collection

- *55 million animal specimens including 28 million insects.*
- *9 million fossils.*
- *6 million plant specimens.*
- *Over 500,000 rocks and minerals.*
- *3,200 meteorites.*

The latest addition to the museum is the Darwin Centre, named after Charles Darwin, the Victorian naturalist, which opened in 2009. The centre contains the museum's most valuable specimen collections in a magnificent cocoon structure and an area where you can watch the scientists working on decoding DNA and preparing specimens.

The Science Museum

Until 1928 the Science Museum was housed within the V&A. In 1931 it opened a children's gallery to encourage and stimulate children's interest in science. This ethos has been at the forefront of the museum ever since and today it continues by using the latest technology for its interactive exhibits. In 2000 the Wellcome Wing, sponsored by the Wellcome Trust, was opened containing present and future science and technology.

Highlights of the Science Museum:

- **Development of Aviation**. This includes Amy Johnson's Gypsy Moth and a British jet.

- **Atmosphere Gallery**. This includes an immersive and interactive gallery that traces the consequences of human action on climate change.

- **Measuring Time**. This contains over 500 timepieces from sundials and water clocks to wristwatches.

- **Exploring Space**. This includes a full-size replica of the 'Eagle' that landed on the moon in 1969.

Pocket Tip 🖊

The Natural History Museum and Science Museum are next door to each other so make time to see both. For more information on opening times and current exhibitions go to the museum websites (www.nhm.ac.uk, www.sciencemuseum.org.uk).

The V&A

The V&A was founded in 1852 and was originally called the Museum of Manufactures. It moved to its present site in 1857, and when Queen Victoria laid the foundation stone for the new façade, it was renamed the Victoria and Albert Museum. The idea behind the museum was to educate working people and inspire British designers and manufacturers. It was one of the earliest museums devoted to the applied or decorative arts. Today it is known simply as the V&A.

Pocket Fact

During the Second World War, many of the museum's exhibits were stored for safety in stone quarries at Bradford-on-Avon.

The V&A's collection spans 2,000 years of human art, manufacture and production including ironwork, jewellery, sculpture, paintings and photographs. It has purchased the original artwork of the Rolling Stones 'lips and tongue' logo designed by John Pasche in 1970 and the remnants of the Gibson Les Paul Goldtop Deluxe guitar belonging to The Who's guitarist Pete Townshend.

Highlights of the V&A:

- **Asia**. Here you will find Tipu's tiger and the Ardabil carpet.

- **Europe**. The British Galleries 1500–1900, includes the Norfolk House music room and Raphael Cartoons 1515

- **Materials and Techniques**. This includes metalwork, furniture, textiles, ceramics, glass, dress, silverwork and theatre and performance. Highlights of these collections include the Luck of Edenhall glass vase, búcaros clay vessels and John Constable's sketchbooks.

Pocket Tip

The V&A has one of the best museum cafés for lunch and opens late during the week. For more details see the museum website (www.vam.ac.uk).

LONDON'S BEST KEPT SECRETS: MUSEUMS

While in London it is not just the world famous museums you should visit. Many smaller museums cover a wide range of interests with wonderful collections of artefacts.

- Imperial War Museum, Lambeth Road

- Churchill War Rooms and Churchill Museum, Clive Steps, King Charles Street

- Hunterian, The Royal College of Surgeons, 35–43 Lincoln Inns Fields

- John Soane Museum, 13 Lincolns Inn Fields

- Transport Museum, Wellington Street

- Geffrye Museum, 136 Kingsland Road

- Pollocks Toy Museum, 25 Scala Street

- Wallace Collection, Manchester Square

- Museum of London, 150 London Wall

- Museum of London Docklands, West India Quay

- Teddy Museum, 240 The Broadway, Wimbledon

- Design Museum, Shad Thames

- Foundling Museum, 40 Brunswick Square

- Museum of Brands, 2–5 Coleville Square

- Garden Museum, Lambeth Palace Road

- Cartoon Museum, 35 Little Russell Street

- Sherlock Holmes Museum, 221b Baker Street

Pocket Tip ▮

For more museums, see the VisitLondon website (www. visitlondon.com/attractions/culture/major-museums).

🚖 ART AND ART GALLERIES 🚖

London has some of the finest art galleries in the world catering for every taste. You can see exhibitions at the Royal Academy, European art at the National Gallery and the Courtauld, British art at Tate Britain and modern and contemporary art at Tate Modern, Saatchi and Whitechapel galleries. From the oldest work of art, a 13th-century English altarpiece at the National Gallery, to Damien Hirst's 20th-century *Mother and Child* at Tate Modern, you can find something that will make you stand back in admiration in any of these galleries.

THE ROYAL ACADEMY

The Royal Academy was founded by George III in 1768. It began with 34 founding members including Sir Joshua Reynolds who, as the first president, established a school of art so the members could pass on their knowledge of drawing, painting, sculpture and architecture to other artists. The academy also provided a venue for artists to exhibit which continues today with the annual summer exhibition, where the Council of Academicians selects 1,200 works from the 10,000 submitted. Almost two-thirds of the works selected are from non-academicians.

Royal academicians

It is an honour for any artist to be recognised by their fellow artists and to be elected a Royal Academician. There are only ever 80 academicians, who must be practising artists and this number must include at least 14 sculptors, 12 architects and eight printmakers with the balance being made up by painters. There can be an unlimited number of senior academicians, who are aged over 75.

Pocket Tip
Look out for the wonderful water feature in the courtyard in front of the Academy.

THE NATIONAL GALLERY

In 1824 the government purchased the art collection of John Julius Angerstein, consisting of 38 paintings. This was to be the core of a national collection which would provide education and enjoyment of art for everyone. The collection was displayed in the house of Angerstein at 100 Pall Mall until a gallery could be built. In 1831 the government provided the funds to build the National Gallery and it opened in 1838. Trafalgar Square was chosen as the most central location so that the well-off living in the West End and the poor living in the East End could visit the gallery easily.

Pocket Fact

Van Gogh's Sunflowers *is the most reproduced painting in the National Gallery, appearing on mouse mats, cards, mugs and posters.*

Today the collection consists of paintings from 1250 to 1900 which include many famous works of art such as the *Wilton Diptych* (1395–1399), the *Arnolfini Portrait* (1434), Van Gogh's *Sunflowers* and works by artists such as Holbein, Bruegal, Rembrandt, Titian, Carravaggio and Cezanne. Go to the gallery's website (www.nationalgallery.org.uk) for more details on opening times and current exhibitions.

Pocket Tip

The entrance through the pillared portico of the National Gallery has the most fantastic mosaics on the floor, including The Labours of Life *and* The Pleasures of Life.

Also try: The Courtauld Gallery

The Courtauld Gallery in Somerset House is part of the Courtauld Institute of Art, one of the world's leading centres for the study of art history and conservation. It is a small gallery with a wonderful collection of paintings from the 14th to the 20th century including altarpieces by Botticelli, *Adam and Eve* by Cranach, portraiture by Gainsborough and one of the finest collections of impressionists and post-impressionists, including paintings and drawings and bronzes by Degas. Go to the gallery's website (www.courtauld.ac.uk) for more details on opening times and current exhibitions.

Pocket Tip 🖋

The gallery is housed in Somerset House so when you are finished in the gallery you can take a walk along the banks of the Thames.

TATE BRITAIN

Tate Britain on Millbank opened in 1897 to house the collection of Henry Tate, the Tate and Lyle sugar magnate. It is dedicated to British art from the 1500s through to today, including a whole wing dedicated to one of Britain's most famous artists J. M. W Turner. The 300 oil paintings and around 30,000 sketches and watercolours works found in Turner's studio on his death formed the 'Turner Bequest' that was left to the nation on the understanding they would be shown in one gallery. The Tate was chosen as its collection is by British artists.

The collection also includes works by Thomas Gainsborough, Joseph Wright of Derby, George Stubbs, Lucien Freud, William Blake, David Hockney and the 'Young British Artists' or YBAs, Tracey Emin and Damien Hirst.

Pocket Tip 🖋

Take the tube to Westminster and walk west along the bank of the River Thames to the Tate Britain. You can also catch a boat up the river to the Tate Modern. Go to the gallery's website (www.tate.org.uk/britain) for more details on opening times and current exhibitions.

TATE MODERN

If you are interested in the weird and the wonderful of the art world, there are a number of galleries in London which specialise in modern and contemporary art.

The Tate Modern is housed in the 1947 Bankside Power Station and the building is a work of art in itself. It was designed by the architects Herzog and De Meuron and their proposal was chosen because it kept as much of the feel and architecture of the old power station as was possible. The massive Turbine Hall is a fantastic entrance into this wonderful gallery of modern and contemporary art from the 1900s including Cézanne, Matisse, Picasso, Rothko, Dalí, Pollock and Warhol. Go to the gallery's website (www.tate.org.uk/modern) for more details on opening times and current exhibitions.

Pocket Tip 🖋

Tate Modern's café-restaurant on the top level has stunning views over the river and City of London.

Also try: the Saatchi Gallery and the Hayward Gallery

The Saatchi Gallery is housed in the Duke of York Headquarters, the old home of the Territorial Army on King's Road. The gallery exhibits contemporary art by young artists and international artists not usually seen in Britain, acting as a springboard to further their careers. Go to the gallery's website (www. saatchi-gallery.co.uk) for more details on opening times and current exhibitions.

The Hayward Gallery is part of the Southbank arts complex on the south bank of the Thames. It hosts three or four exhibitions a year focusing on single artists, historical themes and artistic movements, cultural art and contemporary art. Go to the gallery's website (www.southbankcentre.co.uk/venues/hayward-gallery) for more details on opening times and current exhibitions.

CULTURAL LONDON • 89

London as a work of art

The following are famous paintings which have been inspired by the city, and have captured an aspect of London, providing a pictorial representation of the history of the city.

- The Burning of the Houses of Parliament *(1834) by Turner:* Turner actually witnessed this event and in his painting captures the drama of the destruction of the old medieval buildings.
- Foggy London *series by Monet:* While Monet was in London he painted his famous series of foggy London landscapes, dated 1900 to 1903. In the series Monet painted three views of Charing Cross and Waterloo Bridge and the Houses of Parliament, two looking south from the Savoy Hotel, where he was staying, and one from St Thomas's Hospital looking north. The Thames below Westminster, *dated about 1871, is on display in the National Gallery.*
- Old Battersea Bridge *(1872–1875) by Whistler: This work is on display at Tate Britain.*

🚗 LONDON'S ARTISTIC 🚗 MOVEMENTS

With so many artists living and working in the city, London has always been a hotbed of new ideas which challenged the old order. The Pre-Raphaelites are probably the most well known of these forward thinkers. Founded by William Holman Hunt, Dante Gabriel Rosetti and John Everett Millais in 1848, they wanted to bring back intense colours and abundant detail.

Pocket Fact 🌉

The model for Millais's painting Ophelia *was Elizabeth Siddal, who became seriously ill after he asked her to float in a bath of cold water so he could paint her as the doomed heroine from* Hamlet.

In the 1980s it was the YBAs, which included Tracey Emin and Damien Hirst, who became a force in the world of art. It started with the exhibition 'Freeze' organised by Damien Hirst while still a student at Goldsmiths College. The YBAs believed that anything could be used as a work of art, hence Damien Hirst's preserved dead animals and Tracey Emin's own unmade bed.

Other artistic movements which sprang up in London include:

- Holland Park Circle 1850: Lord Leighton, G.F. Watts, William Burges and Holman Hunt

- New English Art Club 1885: John Singer Sargent, George Clausen, Thomas Cooper Gotch, Philip Wilson Steer and Stanhope Forbes

- Camden Town Group 1911: Walter Sickert, Spencer Gore, Harold Gilman, Robert Bevan and Charles Ginner.

Pocket Fact

London's art scene in the 21st century continues to embrace new ideas and innovation, the latest being the internationally recognised street artist Banksy, whose work can be seen on many London streets. Banksy has also directed his first feature film called Exit Through The Gift Shop, *which portrays the inside story of street art.*

🚕 LONDON THEATRE 🚕

Only in London can one see such a vast array of productions from Shakespeare to original works, to musicals based on blockbuster films, in over 50 theatres. London not only plays host to some wonderful opportunities to enjoy theatre, visitors can also visit venues which have played a significant role in the development of theatre, from Shakespeare's Globe to Drury Lane.

Pocket Tip 🖊

For what's on and information on booking tickets go to the London Theatre website (www.londontheatre.co.uk). You can also try and nab discount tickets from the 'tkts' booth in Leicester Square, operated by the Society of London Theatre, the industry body that represents London theatres.

London's most famous theatres include:

- Shakespeare's Globe Theatre, Southwark: performs original works of Shakespeare.

- The Royal Court, Sloane Square: performs new works by innovative British and international writers.

- National Theatre, South Bank: puts on a mixture of new plays and classics in its three theatres, the Olivier, Lyttelton and Cottesloe.

- The Royal Opera House, Covent Garden: splits its performances between the Royal Ballet and the Royal Opera.

- The Coliseum, Covent Garden: home to the English National Opera, which performs opera in English and is known for its modern interpretations of opera.

- Sadlers Wells, Clerkenwell: dance theatre from contemporary to flamenco, ballet to hip hop.

- The Unicorn Theatre, Tothill Street: champion of children's theatre.

Pocket Tip 🖊

In the summer you can watch live screening of performances by the Royal Ballet and Royal Opera on big screens in Trafalgar Square, Canada Square, Canary Wharf, General Gordon Square, Woolwich and Walthamstow Town Square. For more details go to the View London website (www.viewlondon.co.uk/cinemas/bp-summer-screens-in-london-feature-1066.html).

WEST END THEATRES

The West End theatres began with the Drury Lane Theatre in 1663, Her Majesty's Theatre in 1705, Theatre Royal Haymarket in 1720 and the Royal Opera House in 1731. These were the first theatres built in the area around Covent Garden, an area that was later to become known as 'Theatre Land'.

Myths & Legends 🚌

Drury Lane is said to be one of the most haunted theatres in London. Its most famous ghost is the Man in Grey, a ghost dressed as an 18th-century nobleman. He is said to be the skeletal remains of a man who was stabbed with a knife and found within a walled-up passage in 1848.

In 1843 the Theatres Act gave local authorities the right to license theatres, leading to an explosion in theatre building. These new theatres put on performances by many famous local playwrights such as Oscar Wilde, J. M. Barrie, Henry James and George Bernard Shaw, and since then London theatre has had a reputation for nurturing new talent. The Old Vic, under the directorship of the actor Kevin Spacey, continues London's long tradition of critically acclaimed performances of traditional and cutting edge plays, directed by people such as Trevor Nunn and Sam Mendes and featuring actors such as Kevin Spacey, Tom Hollander and Richard Dreyfus.

Theatres built in the 1880s and 1890s

- *The Shaftesbury, Shaftesbury Avenue.*
- *London Coliseum, St Martin's Lane.*
- *Novello, Aldwych.*
- *Aldwych, Aldwych.*
- *Queen's, Shaftesbury Avenue.*
- *The Palace, Cambridge Circus.*
- *The Lyric, Shaftesbury Avenue.*
- *The Apollo, Shaftesbury Avenue.*
- *The Old Vic, Waterloo.*

THE SOUTH BANK

London continued to build theatres into the 20th century with the building of a new entertainment complex in South Bank to celebrate the Festival of Britain in 1951. This complex contains the National Theatre and music venues including the Royal Festival Hall. In 1982 the Barbican Theatre opened in the City of London as part of the Barbican development.

Pocket Tip

The Royal Festival Hall is on the south bank of the Thames and is a lovely place to relax with a drink and look at the spectacular views of London.

SHAKESPEARE'S GLOBE THEATRE

The most unusual, historic and beautiful theatre to be built in London harks back to the founding days of London's theatres. Shakespeare's Globe opened at Southwark in 1997. The American actor Sam Wanamaker set up the Globe Playhouse Trust in 1970 to try to build a theatre which would celebrate the greatest playwright in the world, William Shakespeare. He drove the project forward consulting with the architect Theo Crosby and leading theatre historians to reconstruct, as closely as possible, a Shakespearian theatre.

Pocket Fact

The Globe is the first building in London to have a thatched roof since the Great Fire of London in 1660. Special permission was given and the thatch is covered in a fire retardant substance and is surrounded by sprinklers.

The theatre is built 250 yards from the site of the original Globe. It is a timber framed building with 15 bays and the walls are covered in a white lime wash. The audience sits around the stage on traditional wooden seats (you can get cushions if you cannot bear this) in tiered bays, or you can stand around the stage, in the open as they did during the 16th century as one of the 'groundlings'.

Pocket Fact 🌉

Sam Wanamaker never saw his theatre completed as he died in 1993 when only 12 of the 15 bays were completed.

🚕 LONDON FILM LOCATIONS 🚕

London is very popular with filmmakers; its wonderful buildings provide unique locations and its wealth of history and the diversity of its people provide endless topics for both film and television scripts. Its buildings can often double as a variety of locations, from St Bartholomew-the-Great, which appeared as Nottingham Castle in *Robin Hood: Prince of Thieves*, to Leadenhall Market, which was used in the Harry Potter films.

Top London film locations

See if you can spot the following locations in the films listed alongside.

- **St Bartholomew-the-Great, Smithfield**. Four Weddings and a Funeral, Shakespeare in Love, Elizabeth: The Golden Age, Amazing Grace *and* Robin Hood: Prince of Thieves.
- **Royal Naval College, Greenwich**. Four Weddings and a Funeral, Sherlock Holmes, The Madness of King George, The Golden Compass, The Young Victoria, Lara Croft: Tomb Raider, The Mummy *and* The Queen.
- **Somerset House, Strand**. The Duchess, Golden Eye, Tomorrow Never Dies *and* Shanghai Knights.
- **The River Thames and the iconic London landmarks along the river**. Golden Eye *and* Love Actually.

🚖 FILMS ABOUT LONDON 🚖

London is a great subject for film: from its long and varied history to the variety and character of its people. It has a wealth of subject matter perfect for any film-maker. Just like other big cities London has its seedier side which also makes for fantastic scripts, while some of London's landmarks make the perfect setting for some of the most romantic moments seen on the big screen.

Gangster London

Lock Stock and Two Smoking Barrels (1998), *Snatch* (2000) and *Rock n Rolla* (2008), directed by Guy Ritchie, show a side of London that the majority of people do not see. These films are excellent at portraying the dark humour that is typical of Londoners.

Trendy London

Notting Hill (1999) captures the area around West London perfectly with its mixture of markets and trendy and independent shops. The drive to the Savoy at the end of the film through London streets is wonderful even if they have taken artistic licence with the route: to drive from the Haymarket to the Savoy you would go straight around to Trafalgar Square and not from the Haymarket to the Mall and then around Trafalgar Square.

Bridget Jones' Diary (2001) shows the lifestyle of London's unattached thirty-somethings. The film locations include Borough Market, where Bridget has a flat over the Globe Pub. The long lingering kiss at the end of the film takes place at the Royal Exchange, although how Bridget ran from Borough Market to the Royal Exchange, a distance of over half a mile, in one minute in her underwear is a mystery!

Historical London

Shakespeare in Love (1998) portrays the life of Shakespeare and how theatre was at the edge of polite society in Elizabethan London. London locations used for this film were St Bartholomew the Great, Spitalfields and Whitehall.

Bells Go Down (1943) is famous for its depiction of London during the Second World War. The film incorporates documentary footage as the backdrop to the lives of London firemen and their families during the Blitz.

The King's Speech (2010) takes place in the period just before the abdication crisis of Edward VIII in 1936 after the Depression, when London appears as a dark and grimy place. The film uses a variety of locations around London such as 33 Portland Place as the home of the Duke and Duchess at 145 Piccadilly, and Iliffe Street, Elephant & Castle, the home of Lionel Logue.

Filming locations for Harry Potter

One of the biggest film franchises of the past century, Harry Potter, used several London locations, which eager fans can track down to relive their favourite moments.

- *Leadenhall Market: entrance to Leaky Cauldron.*
- *King's Cross Station: Platform $9\frac{3}{4}$.*
- *Foyer of Australia House: Gringotts Bank.*
- *St Pancras Station: Harry and Ron fly by in Mr Weasley's car.*
- *Great Scotland Yard: entrance to Ministry of Magic.*
- *Westminster Underground station: Harry and Mr Weasley get stuck in the ticket barriers.*
- *River Thames: Harry and the Order of the Phoenix travel up the river on broomsticks.*
- *Millennium Bridge: the bridge is attacked by the Death Eaters.*

CINEMA IN LONDON

The London cinema scene is also vibrant, providing a number of venues both indoors and outdoors where you can watch a large range of films from black and white silent movies to the latest blockbusters.

Pocket Fact ⚓

The smallest cinema in London is the Southbank Studio with 38 seats, and the largest is the Odeon Leicester Square with 1,679 seats.

The National Film Theatre

The National Film Theatre, more simply known as the NFT, is located on the South Bank and is run by the British Film Institute. It puts on a monthly programme of films that focus on specific directors, actors, countries, genres and television catering to a huge range of ages and tastes. The theatre also runs question and answer sessions with directors and is the place to go for classic black and white films and foreign art house movies. Visit the British Film Institute's website (www.bfi.org.uk) for more information on what's on at the NFT.

A typical programme at the NFT

- *Season of Fred Astaire and Ginger Rogers.*
- *The television work of Julie Walters.*
- *The Disney 50.*
- *Films celebrating Britain's shipbuilding.*
- *François Truffaut, the influential French director.*

Other cool cinemas in London

- The Electric Cinema, Portobello Road: one of London's oldest cinemas, there are side tables, armchairs and a bar at the back of the cinema to make this a luxurious experience.

- Everyman Cinema Club, Hampstead: sofas and drinks are complemented by snacks such as bread and olive oil, and you can join the members' club to attend special screenings.

- Curzon, Soho: situated on Shaftesbury Avenue, this is London's best independent cinema showing a range of art house films.

- Prince Charles Cinema, Leicester Square: this is the place to go for cheap tickets and special sing-a-long screenings and double bills.

- BFI IMAX, South Bank: home to the biggest cinema screen in the UK, the IMAX is the place to experience blockbusters and specially made nature films.

OUTDOOR SCREENINGS

When watching films outside in London you have the added bonus of the view around the screen as many of are located in historic settings or with wonderful views.

For the best outdoor cinema try:

- Somerset House, Strand

- The Scoop, City Hall

- Dulwich Picture Gallery

- NFT South Bank.

Pocket Fact 🌉

Secret cinema is a new phenomenon that screens films in themed locations which are kept secret until the last minute and cryptic clues are given as to the dress code. For more information go to the Secret Cinema website (www.secretcinema.org).

🚗 TELEVISION AND LONDON 🚗

London and Londoners are as popular in television as they are in film. Some programmes such as *EastEnders*, portray the lives of Londoners (even though they are not actually filmed in London!), while others use London as a backdrop to add to the drama and excitement of the storylines, such as *Spooks* which uses the streets of London as the setting for the drama about the British security service.

EastEnders

This popular soap is about the domestic and professional lives of a group of people living in a fictional East End borough, but it is actually recorded at the BBC studios about 25 miles away from London in Elstree in Hertfordshire. The tube station in the programme, Walford East, does not exist but on the tube map on the wall of the station it is on the District and Hammersmith & City lines and replaces Bromley by Bow.

Pocket Fact

The outdoor scenes of the archetypal series about Londoners Only Fools and Horses *were mainly filmed in Bristol.*

Some television programmes filmed in London

- *Goodnight Sweetheart*: Bethnal Green.

- *Absolutely Fabulous*: Holland Park, Harvey Nichols, Knightsbridge.

- *Spooks*: Freemasons Hall, Covent Garden and Shoreditch.

- *Sherlock*: North Gower Street.

- *Ashes to Ashes*: Silwood Street, Bermondsey and the River Thames.

- *Dr Who*: Westminster Bridge, Tower of London, Baltic House, Houses of Parliament.

- *Minder*: Royal Albert Hall, Notting Hill, Hammersmith and Fulham Police Station.

- *Grange Hill*: Kingsbury, north-west London.

- *The Bill*: Merton, south-west London and Docklands.

- *The Sweeney*: Battersea, Chelsea, Chiswick and Hammersmith.

- *Rumpole of the Bailey*: Temple, Holborn.

🚕 LONDON'S MUSIC SCENE 🚕

London has always inspired a vibrant and varied range of music. From Handel to Hendrix, in London you can listen to any kind of live music you want, including classical, rock, country and folk, jazz, indie and hip hop. The city has also been the birthplace of a huge number of legendary artists and musical movements.

Pocket Fact 🌉

In 1968 Jimi Hendrix lived at 23 Brook Street and in the 18th century Handel lived next door at No. 25, which is now the Handel Museum.

MUSICAL GENRES FROM LONDON

London's pulsating music scene, with its plethora of large and small venues, has resulted in it being a breeding ground for constantly changing and developing musical genres. London musicians took American rock music and developed it into punk and glam rock, American garage music became grime and Jamaican ska evolved into English Two Tone.

Punk music

Punk music, already part of the New York underground music scene, was founded in London in the 1970s by Malcolm McLaren. He was looking for a new front man for the band he was managing. He chose John Lydon, aka Johnny Rotten, and the Sex Pistols were born. Punk music struck a chord with the young – it was rebellious and different from the rock music scene which they felt had been high-jacked by the over-25s.

Pocket Fact 🌉

In 1977 the Sex Pistols and McLaren were arrested for playing their new release God Save the Queen *from a hired boat on the river outside the Houses of Parliament.*

Within a year the punk scene was huge and it inspired other groups such as The Clash from West London. The Clash formed in 1976 and incorporated a number of musical genres in its music including reggae, ska, dub, funk and traditional rock and roll to give it its unique sound. The band was known for its politicised lyrics and rebellious attitude and the lyrics appealed to the British youth as the group did not sing about Californian beaches but the band members' own lives in West London.

Other influential artists born in London

- *Amy Winehouse: Southgate.*
- *Lily Allen: Hammersmith.*
- *David Bowie: Brixton.*
- *Adele: Tottenham.*
- *Tinie Tempah: Plumstead*
- *Seal: Paddington.*

Grime

UK Grime is a musical genre that developed out of London's underground music scene in the early 2000s. Many performers gained their reputation by being played on pirate radio stations before becoming 'mainstream'. The most famous exponent of this genre of music is Dizzee Rascal, born in Bow, who has achieved worldwide acclaim.

LONDON'S BEST MUSIC VENUES

London's music venues cover a wide range of music from classical at the Royal Festival Hall to club music at the Ministry of Sound. In London there is a venue for whatever you want to listen to.

- **Royal Festival Hall, South Bank**. This is a popular venue for classical music.

- **Barbican Centre, Silk Street**. This is the home of the London Symphony Orchestra.

- **Marquee Club, Oxford Street**. This pop music venue has seen the likes of Rolling Stones, Jimi Hendrix, David Bowie and Genesis, The Clash, The Police and Joy Division.

- **O2 Arena, Greenwich**. The former Millennium Dome has been transformed into a highly popular entertainment venue which has seen the likes of Lady Gaga, Coldplay, Kings of Leon and even live performances of the *Star Wars* soundtrack played by the Royal Philharmonic Orchestra.

- **Hyde Park**. A popular venue for outdoor concerts including Proms in the Park and the Wireless Festival.

- **O2 Academy, Brixton**. As popular with bands as it is with audiences, the Brixton Academy is excellent for live music from past favourites to up and coming bands playing reggae, funk, rock and pop music. Acts that have performed at the Academy include Bob Dylan, Rolling Stones, Prince, Bruce Springsteen, Primal Scream, Radiohead, The Foo Fighters, Coldplay, Moby, Eminem, Travis and REM.

- **The Ministry of Sound, 103 Gaunt Street**. Although not a live music venue, the Ministry of Sound has gained a world-wide reputation for its DJs and club music, releasing many albums. It now has an associated record label promoting new singers and songwriters.

- **Royal Albert Hall, Kensington Gore**. The Promenade Concerts or 'Proms' have been held here since 1941. These are an annual series of orchestral music concerts that run for eight weeks at the Royal Albert Hall, covering a wide variety of tastes. Visit the BBC Proms website (www.bbc.co.uk/proms) for more information.

- **Ronnie Scott's, 47 Frith Street**. Legendary jazz club with performances by jazz, rhythm and blues and soul musicians that include Madeline Bell, Jack Bruce and Dee Dee Bridgewater.

- **Madame JoJo's, 8–10 Brewer Street**. This has a wide selection of club nights playing anything from 1960s and 1970s to Jump and Jive and Rockabilly to Latin and disco.

- **Electric Ballroom, 148 Camden High Street**. Opened over 40 years ago, this has a wide variety of club music nights playing hard rock, ska, punk and disco. Live music has included Madness, The Clash, George Thorogood and the Smiths and recent performances by The Killers, The Raconteurs, AFI, Gogol Bordello and Paul McCartney

- **The Roundhouse, Chalk Farm Road**. From choir music to dub step music by Chase and Status, the Roundhouse has an eclectic programme of live music.

MUSIC STUDIOS

There are many music studios in London, including Air Studios where Katie Melua, Susan Boyle, Paolo Nutini and Paloma Faith recorded, and Trident, whose artists included Elton John, David Bowie, Black Sabbath and Queen. However, the most famous is Abbey Road in Hampstead where the Beatles recorded their *Abbey Road* album.

Pocket Fact 🌉

The Abbey Road zebra crossing is the most photographed in the world as everyone wants to copy the famous Beatles album cover. The local authority has now moved the road sign beyond the reach of souvenir hunters.

Other artists who have also recorded at Abbey Road include Cliff Richard, Pink Floyd, Kate Bush, Duran Duran and Radiohead.

Songs about London

London has not only played host to some great live music but has also inspired some classic songs:

- London Calling, *The Clash.*
- Down in the Tube Station at Midnight, *The Jam.*
- Waterloo Sunset, *The Kinks.*

- LDN, *Lily Allen*.
- Streets of London, *Ralph McTell*.
- West End Girls, *Pet Shop Boys*.
- Werewolves of London, *Warren Zevon*.
- Mile End, *Pulp*.
- A Foggy Day in London Town, *Ella Fitzgerald*.

LONDON RECORD LABELS

With such a varied music scene it is only to be expected that London should also have a variety of record labels from large corporate labels such as EMI (The Electric and Musical Industries Ltd) to independent record labels such as XL Recordings and Rough Trade Records.

EMI

EMI opened its first recording studios at Abbey Road in 1931 and went on to record such artists as Edward Elgar and Otto Klemperer. The 1950s to 1970s were its heyday as its recording artists included Frank Sinatra, The Beatles, The Hollies, Cliff Richard, Pink Floyd and Queen. In 1996 EMI signed the Spice Girls and has continued with artists such as Corinne Bailey Rae, Tinie Tempah and Gorillaz.

Pocket Fact ◀▙▶

The stairwell of EMI's Manchester Street headquarters is on the cover of the Beatles album Please Please Me.

XL Records

XL Records was founded by Richard Russell with Beggars Banquet Records and initially recorded rave and dance music with artists such as The Prodigy and then went on to record artists such as Dizzee Rascal, Basement Jazz and Badly Drawn Boy.

Rough Trade Records

Rough Trade Records was founded in 1978 by Geoff Travis out of his Rough Trade record shop in West London. Rough Trade's first release was by a French punk band called Metal Urbaine and by 1979 it had its first major success with Stiff Little Fingers' *Inflammable Material*, which was the first independent record label to sell over 100,000 copies. In 1984 the label signed The Smiths and after some financial problems in the 1990s has continued to develop recording artists such as Jarvis Cocker, The Libertines and Antony & The Johnsons.

Pocket Fact ⚓

Richard Branson's empire was started in 1972 with a small record shop called Virgin Records in Notting Hill, which offered bean bags and free vegetarian food to its customers.

6

FASHIONABLE LONDON

If you walk the streets of London you can easily see why it is one of the fashion capitals of the world. You'll see every kind of fashion trend imaginable, from the typical English look of Sloane Street to the latest urban fashion of the East End. From the 17th century the man about town would buy the latest designs from the men's outfitters around St James's and in the 1960s fashion became Britain's most spectacular export. Today it is the up and coming designers of the London's East End who set the latest fashion trends. This chapter will guide you through London fashion, covering how fashionable London has developed as well as exploring some of the best shopping areas that make London such a great place for fashion.

🚕 HISTORY OF FASHION 🚕

ST JAMES'S AND JERMYN STREET

One of the earliest fashion districts of London was St James's. In the 17th century the upper-class gentleman would leave his country estate to visit London to see to his business interests. It was important that he was dressed in the latest fashion and a number of shops sprang up around the gentlemen's clubs in St James's to cater for the man about town.

Pocket Fact 🌉

There is a statue of Beau Brummell in Jermyn Street. He was the arbiter of 18th-century London fashion, and everyone, including the Prince Regent, copied him. Brummell is credited with introducing full-length trousers which replaced knee-length breeches.

St James's supplied all a man might need, from his hat at Lock & Co (where the first bowler hat was sold) to his shoes at Lobbs (where the first Wellington boot was made). Today Jermyn Street is still renowned for its bespoke tailoring, shoes, shirts and luxury goods. The shirtmakers Turnbull & Asser in Jermyn Street have made shirts for every actor who has played James Bond from Sean Connery to Daniel Craig.

1960s LONDON FASHION

In the 1960s a fashion revolution took place. Fashion designers became celebrities as their clothes were manufactured en masse and boutique shopping became popular. Until the late 1950s there were no clothes designed specifically for young people but in 1955 Mary Quant opened her boutique Bazaar in King's Road, showcasing her simple daisy motif, short skirts, hot pants, the slip dress and PVC raincoats. Her designs soon came to epitomise the swinging sixties London scene. London became the place the world looked to for the latest trends.

Pocket Fact ⟞⊓⟝

London-born Twiggy, discovered at the tender age of 16, became synonymous with the fashion of the 1960s and Mary Quant's designs. As the first international supermodel, her stick thin androgynous look set the standard for every supermodel.

Meanwhile Biba, started by Barbara Hulanicki, opened its first store in Kensington in 1964. It was completely different from the bright designs of Mary Quant with dresses in blackish mulberries, blueberries, rusts and plum colours. Biba became popular with young people as they could wear the same clothes as they had seen on their fashion and pop icons such as Mick Jagger and Marianne Faithful.

Pocket Fact ◢▟▙◣

Supermodels Kate Moss, Naomi Campbell, Jade Parfitt, Lily Cole and Daisy Lowe all grew up in London.

MODERN LONDON FASHION

Today it is London's East End that is setting the trends. In the 1980s this area became trendy when Tracey Emin, Damien Hirst, Alexander McQueen and the White Cube Gallery moved into what was a cheap and rundown area of London. Now it is home to cafés, bars, restaurants, shops and the studios of the latest designers, such as Marios Schwab, Henry Holland, Richard Nicholl and Christopher Kane.

Pocket Fact ◢▟▙◣

Central St Martins College of Art and Design is one of the reasons that London remains a centre of innovative fashion design. Its students have included John Galliano, Katherine Hamnett, Stella McCartney and Alexander McQueen.

East End fashionistas

As the East End became synonymous with fashion, the area became famous not just for its designers but for the group of East End fashionistas who wear up-to-the-minute, cutting edge designs and set the fashion trends around London.

Where to see the East End fashionistas

- *Spitalfields Market.*
- *Brick Lane.*
- *Hoxton Square.*
- *Truman Brewery.*

🚗 LONDON'S DESIGNERS 🚗

London has inspired some of the most cutting edge fashion designers who have created trends and caused controversy. Here are just a few of them.

VIVIENNE WESTWOOD

Vivienne Westwood started designing during the 1970s and in 1976 put London at the forefront of both fashion and music trends when she opened a shop called Let it Rock with Malcolm McLaren of the Sex Pistols. Vivienne's designs were rebellious and bucked the popular hippie years of the 1970s. Vivienne designed Rock 'n' Roll fashion and constantly pushed the boundaries of fashion trends. Since 1984 Vivienne Westwood has changed direction from the street-style youth culture designs of her early career and now finds inspiration in Savile Row tailoring techniques, British fabrics and 17th- and 18th-century art.

Pocket Fact 🌉

In 2004 the V&A held a retrospective exhibition of Vivienne Westwood to celebrate 34 years of her designs. It was the largest exhibition ever hosted by a designer and cemented her reputation as one of the most influential designers in the world.

OZWALD BOATENG

Ozwald Boateng trained as a tailor in Savile Row and he has united this skill with his own unique approach to design to create menswear that is stylish and beautiful. He opened his first studio in Portobello Road in 1991 and quickly found success with his contemporary approach to design. He was the first tailor to stage a catwalk show in Paris in 1994. He moved to Vigo Street in 1995 and was mentored by the avant-garde men's tailor, Tommy Nutter.

Tommy Nutter, who was famous for reinventing the Savile Row suit in the 1960s, designed suits for many famous people including Elton John and Mick Jagger but his biggest claim to fame was that he designed the suits worn by Paul McCartney, John Lennon and Ringo Starr for the cover of the *Abbey Road* album. George Harrison wore his jeans and denim jacket.

In 2002 Ozwald moved into Savile Row and is credited with bringing a new generation of men to Savile Row tailoring. He is also one of the pioneers of the new bespoke couture movement in men's clothing with clients such as Robbie Williams, Will Smith and Samuel L. Jackson.

STELLA MCCARTNEY

In 1995 Stella McCartney's graduation show at Central St Martins College of Art and Design was modelled by her friends Kate Moss, Naomi Campbell and Yasmin Le Bon. It was an auspicious start for this now internationally famous designer. In 1997 after only two collections she became the creative director of the house of Chloe in Paris. Her designs combine sharp tailoring with humour (such as her fruity vests and knickers) and sexy femininity, and have made Chloe a huge commercial success.

Pocket Fact 🌉

Stella McCartney is a vegetarian and has famously managed to be successful without using any fur or leather.

In 2001 Stella launched her own fashion house in a joint venture with Gucci and has now branched out into a women's ready-to-wear line, accessories, lingerie, eyewear, fragrance, children's clothes and an organic skincare range. She has also collaborated with Adidas on a sportswear collection which has led to her appointment as the creative director for Team GB's official kit across all disciplines for the 2012 Olympics and Paralympics.

ALEXANDER MCQUEEN

Alexander McQueen was one of the most internationally acclaimed London designers. He gained an infamous reputation from his collections which used shock tactics and controversy and was described as the '*enfant terrible*' and 'the hooligan of English fashion'. McQueen graduated in 1991 from Central St Martins College of Art and Design, having been accepted by the director on his portfolio alone. He opened his first studio in the East End in 1992 and was appointed chief designer at Givenchy in 1996. His collections combined the skills he learnt in London's Savile Row, fine workmanship of French haute couture and finishing of Italian manufacturing.

Myths & Legends

While working in Savile Row, one of McQueen's clients was Prince Charles and it is rumoured that he scrawled 'McQueen was here' inside the lining of his suit.

Following McQueen's death on 11 February 2010, Anna Wintour of US *Vogue* magazine described him as transporting his followers 'into a world of sensation where you could be shocked, repulsed or thrilled'.

LONDON FASHION WEEK

London Fashion Week is now considered one of the 'Big Four' fashion weeks along with Paris, Milan and New York. Taking place twice a year in February and September, it is organised by the British Fashion Council for the London Development Agency. It started in 1984 in a West London car park but since then the organisers have chosen iconic London venues for the main events, and over the years it has been held at the Natural History Museum and Somerset House. Each designer holds their catwalk show at a number of venues throughout the city.

London Fashion Week has seen the debut of many famous fashion designers including Betty Jackson, Ghost, John Galliano, Stella McCartney, Christopher Kane, handbag designer Anya Hindmarch and the latest young London designer Rhiannon Jones, whose collection has been worn by Lady Gaga. The London

Fashion Week features the collections of over 170 designers and is visited by more than 5,000 press and buyers.

Pocket Tip 🖊

You can now watch London Fashion Week from the comfort of your home as there is a live video stream at www.londonfashionweeklive.co.uk.

LONDON FASHION WEEKEND

London Fashion Weekend takes place the weekend after London Fashion Week and is open to the public. The event includes catwalk shows, fashion, hair care and beauty tips and an opportunity to preview up and coming trends. There is also the opportunity to buy designer shopping from over 100 brands at discounts of up to 70%. Tickets are available online at its website (www.londonfashionweekend.co.uk).

🚗 BEST SHOPPING AREAS 🚗 IN LONDON

London has a wide variety of shopping districts which sell clothes, from designer labels such as Dior and cutting-edge fashion by young designers to bargain clothes at markets. Here we'll look at some of the best shopping areas in London.

FOR UPMARKET SHOPPING

Knightsbridge and Sloane Street

Home to Harvey Nichols and Harrods and fabulous designer shops, this area caters for all tastes and also has high street labels such as Topshop. But it is renowned for its prestigious brands including designer labels such as Armani, Burberry, Louis Vuitton, MiuMiu, Versace and Hermes. The nearest tube is Knightsbridge.

Harrods

With its motto 'All Things for All People, Everywhere', Harrods can claim to be one of the most famous department stores in the world. It was founded in 1849 selling mostly tea and groceries but has now grown to seven floors and 330 departments of shopping, including six food halls. The nearest tube is Knightsbridge.

Pocket Tip

Visit the amazing Egyptian staircase in Harrods with its gold pharaoh statues.

Harvey Nichols

Opened in 1813 as a linen shop, Harvey Nichols has become a shopping mecca. Affectionately known as 'Harvey Nicks', it has eight floors of fashion, beauty and lifestyle and is great for latest designer labels. The nearest tube is Knightsbridge.

Bond Street and New Bond Street

Home to stores such as Tiffany, Harry Winston, Calvin Klein and Alexander McQueen, this is the most exclusive area for high-end shopping for fashion, art and antiques. The nearest tube is Bond Street.

Pocket Tip

Bond Street is a great place to window shop and marvel at the diamonds.

Mayfair

Home to the world famous Savile Row, this area is the home of bespoke men's tailoring where you can shop for handmade suits from tailors such as Henry Poole & Co, Ozwald Boateng, Gieves and Hawkes, and Richard Anderson. The nearest tube stations are Green Park and Oxford Circus.

Pocket Fact ⬫

Savile Row's claim to fame is not just its tailoring, as No. 3 Savile Row was where The Beatles gave their rooftop concert at the end of the film Let It Be.

Regent Street

Home to Liberty, the world famous Hamleys toy store and traditional British stores Jaeger and Aquascutum, Regent Street is a mixture of high street and upmarket brands such as Oasis, Topshop, All Saints, H&M and Karen Millen. The nearest tube is Oxford Circus.

Liberty

Opened in 1875 Liberty is a wonderful shop with wood panelling, selling its famous Liberty fabrics, classic and contemporary designs, luxury goods and furniture.

Pocket Fact ⬫

In 1878 Liberty commissioned its first Liberty art fabric, a tradition it continues today, using up-and-coming and award-winning illustrators.

Piccadilly and Jermyn Street

Home to Fortnum & Mason, and two of the oldest men's shops in London, this is one of the oldest shopping areas of London. Here you will find Russell & Hodge (bespoke shirtmakers), John Lobb (19th-century bootmakers), and you can also buy wine at the 17th-century Berry Bros & Rudd and cigars at Fox of St James's, which supplied cigars to Winston Churchill. The nearest tube is Green Park.

Fortnum & Mason

Established in 1705 by Hugh Mason and William Fortnum, this is the place for luxurious food shopping and homeware where you are served by staff in tailcoats. The store is world famous for its toiletries, ladies' fashion accessories, toys, luggage and men's accessories.

Pocket Tip

Look out for the clock striking the hour outside the door when Mr Fortnum and Mr Mason come out and bow to each other.

Oxford Street

Home to Selfridges and other British department and high street stores, Oxford Street is considered by many to be a shopper's paradise with a mixture of stores including Debenhams, House of Fraser, John Lewis and Marks & Spencer. The nearest stations are Oxford Circus, Bond Street and Marble Arch.

Selfridges

Opened in 1909 by the American Gordon Selfridge, it was voted the best department store in the world. Selfridges's 27 windows have become as famous as the store with their constantly changing displays, showing current designs, styling and fashion trends, and their themed displays at Christmas.

FOR CUTTING EDGE FASHION

Hoxton Square

Home to the Hoxton Boutique, this is the place for up-to-the-minute designs in the latest trendsetting area of London. Hoxton Boutique is a gallery-type store with independent retailers that sell unique and original labels from around the world including Paul & Joe, Sister, MM6 and Kaori. The nearest tubes are Old Street and Liverpool Street.

Pocket Tip

Hoxton Square has a great selection of bars and restaurants including the well-known Hoxton Bar & Kitchen.

Shoreditch

Shoreditch has a huge variety of shops with anything from hip hop clothes to designer and vintage wear. Wholesome sells hip hop influenced menswear including baggy tees and Supra trainers. At Start you can buy the latest designs in handbags, tights, jewellery and clothes, and its latest venture is its own tailoring line. The shop Paper Dress Vintage sells vintage clothing, shoes and accessories from 1900 to 1980s and it has a team on site to alter the clothes to suit. You can even hire the clothes for parties or events. The nearest tube is Old Street.

FOR MARKET SHOPPING

Old Spitalfields market

This old Victorian market area has shops around the market, but the biggest draw is the market stalls, selling fashion from designers and artists to resellers, as well as original artwork, records, books and a great selection of antiques. The nearest tube is Liverpool Street.

Market days are as follows:

- Monday to Wednesday: all shops and no stalls.

- Thursday: antiques and vintage.

- Friday: fashion and art.

- Saturday: all shops and no stalls.

- Sunday: all stalls and shops are open but this is the busiest day.

Camden market

Camden market is famous for its unusual stalls with vintage clothes, antiques, retro T-shirts, crafty goods and furniture. Look out for The Black Rose shop selling Goth, burlesque, corsets, stockings and menswear, A Dandy in Aspic selling retro finds from 1950s, 1960s and 1970s, and Brian's Classic Luggage etc sells a mix of old suitcases, cameras, sportswear and telephones. The nearest tube is Camden Town.

Pocket Tip ❚

Camden market is open throughout the week from 11am to 6pm with the exception of the Electric Ballroom market, which opens on Sundays only. The Camden Canal market and the antiques section of the Stables market are only open at weekends from 11am to 6pm.

Brick Lane

On a visit to Brick Lane you can either walk along the streets visiting the shops and stalls or pop into the old Truman Brewery. The Laden Store sells independent designers and the Rokit Store is great for vintage clothing. In the Truman Brewery you will find Maria Zureta Bijoux selling antique and designer jewellery and Junky Styling is an innovative recycled clothing label. The nearest tubes are Aldgate East and Liverpool Street.

Pocket Tip ❚

Brick Lane market is open on Sundays only from 8am to 2pm. In the Truman Brewery the Backyard market opens every Saturday 11am to 6pm and every Sunday 10am to 5pm.

Portobello Road

There is a variety of stalls selling everything from antique furniture to bananas. The antique stalls sell a selection of vintage clothing, handbags, lace and jewellery and the fashion stalls sell everything from second-hand clothes to young designers trying to get their designs out there. There are some fashion stores including Paul Smith, Myla and Joseph. Portobello Road is the main section for fashion but you will find other clothing stalls dotted about the market. The nearest tube is Notting Hill Gate, or Ladbroke Grove for the fashion end of the market.

Burlington Arcade

There are a number of arcades in Piccadilly that boast some of the most wonderful independent shops, including the Royal Arcade, Piccadilly Arcade and the Princes Arcade. However, the most famous and beautiful is the Regency-style Burlington Arcade next to the Royal Academy. It was built in 1819 and is home to a variety of little shops that look like something out of a Dickensian novel. The arcade has its own private police force, 'the Beadle', dressed in their distinctive navy uniform with a top hat. They enforce a number of rules which state that there can be:

- *no running*
- *no singing*
- *no humming*
- *no riding*
- *no carrying of an unfurled umbrella.*

The arcade is open every day and the nearest tubes are Green Park and Piccadilly Circus.

🚕 ROYAL WARRANTS 🚕

The ultimate accolade for a shop is that it supplies goods to members of the royal family. This is recognised by the granting of a royal warrant, awarded when a company or individual has supplied goods and services for at least five years to Her Majesty The Queen, His Royal Highness The Duke of Edinburgh or His Royal Highness The Prince of Wales. The company is then allowed to display the warrant on its products, premises, stationery and advertising, and it can display the royal coat of arms of the member of the royal family along with the statement 'By Royal Appointment'. There are currently around 850 royal warrant holders and they have to uphold a high standard of service and excellence. Royal warrants can be cancelled and are removed five years after the death of the royal who granted the warrant.

Some royal warrant holders

- *Weetabix: breakfast cereal.*
- *Unitech Complete Computing: bespoke software and information technology.*
- *Charbonnel et Walker: hot chocolate powder and chocolates.*
- *Swaine Adeney & Brigg: carriages, riding whips and saddles.*
- *Rigby & Peller: lingerie.*
- *Floris: perfumes and toiletries.*

7

OUTDOOR LONDON

London is a great place to spend time outdoors. With 40% of Greater London covered by parks and public gardens there is a lot more outdoor space than you would expect in such a busy city. London is also home to some of the most famous sporting occasions in the world, such as Wimbledon and the London Marathon. This chapter will tell you all about London's green spaces, how they have developed and what you can do there. It will trace the history of the Thames, as well as providing a guide to some of the sporting events that take place in London.

🚗 LONDON'S PARKS 🚗

London is awash with parks, an unusual trait for such a large city. Most of these parks began as hunting grounds for the monarchy, including Hyde Park, Green Park, St James's Park, Regent's Park, Greenwich Park, Richmond Park and Bushy Park. In addition, London has a number of other open spaces including Kensington Gardens, Kew Gardens and Battersea Park. Hampstead Heath, to the north of London, was originally common land and, along with Richmond Park, provides the most natural open space you can visit in London. The Royal Parks is the organisation that manages the 5,000 acres of parks on behalf of the monarch. For more information on highlights of the parks, picnic tips and cycling routes, go to the Royal Parks website (www.royalparks.gov.uk).

Pocket Fact 🌉

The views of St Paul's Cathedral in the City of London from Hampstead Heath and Richmond Park are two of the 10 protected views stopping high buildings being built around the cathedral.

London's central parks include:

- Hyde Park
- St James's Park
- Green Park
- Kensington Gardens
- Regent's Park and Primrose Hill.

These parks cover a total of 729 acres and have affectionately been dubbed the 'lungs of London'. They cover such a large area that you can walk across central London from St James's Park in the east to Kensington Palace in the west (a distance of about 3 miles) without leaving the parks.

HYDE PARK

Hyde Park has been opened permanently to the public since the 1600s and today is very popular with walkers, horse riders and cyclists. You can even hire boats or feed the ducks on the Serpentine Lake. Every year on Christmas Day there is a swimming race in the Serpentine for the Peter Pan Cup. The Cup is named after Peter Pan because J. M. Barrie, the author of *Peter Pan*, presented the cup in 1904.

Hyde Park will be the venue for the Triathlon and Swimming Marathon during the London Olympics in 2012.

Pocket Tip

Look out for the Princess Diana Memorial Fountain opened in 2004 on the south bank of the Serpentine Lake. It's a nice place to cool off on a hot day. The nearest tube stations are Green Park and Hyde Park Corner.

ST JAMES'S PARK

St James's Park is the smallest park in the centre of London and was created as a hunting ground when Henry VIII built St James's

Palace in the 16th century. Charles II remodelled it in the 17th century and opened it to the public. It is here that you can find Buckingham Palace, St James's Palace, The Mall and Horse Guards Parade. The wildfowl pond is very popular with a wide variety of species, including pelicans.

Pocket Tip

For good food and great views the lakeside Inn the Park (www.innthepark.com) is well worth a visit. The nearest tube stations are St James's Park, Green Park and Charing Cross.

At the 2012 Olympics, the Mall next to St James's Park will be the start and finish of the road cycling and the Olympic and Paralympics marathon and race walk.

GREEN PARK

The first recorded mention of Green Park was in 1554 when it was known as Upper St James's Park. It was enclosed by Charles II in 1668 and stocked with deer for hunting. In 1726 it was renamed Green Park and in 1826 was opened to the public. Legend has it that Green Park got its name because Catherine of Braganza, wife of Charles II, stopped flowers being planted so that the King would not pick them for any of his 12 mistresses.

Pocket Tip

Today the 'green' park has over 25,000 bulbs in springtime, which burst into bloom creating a sea of yellow. Deckchairs are available for hire in the park; for more details go to the website (www.parkdeckchairs.co.uk). The nearest tube stations are Green Park and Hyde Park Corner.

KENSINGTON GARDENS

Kensington Gardens was originally part of Hyde Park but when Kensington Palace became the home of William III, part of it was used to create the gardens of the palace. It was Queen Caroline, the wife of George II, who created the garden we see today made up of formal avenues of trees, lovely flower beds, the Long Water and Serpentine Lake. The statue of Peter Pan in Kensington Gardens was paid for by J. M. Barrie, the author of *Peter Pan*, who put it up overnight on the spot where, in the story, Peter Pan lands beside the Long Water after flying out of his nursery. This meant that the statue was suddenly present in the park the next morning as if by magic.

REGENT'S PARK AND PRIMROSE HILL

Regent's Park is considered to be the 'jewel in the crown' of the royal parks. It was originally called Marylebone Park but in 1811 was renamed after the Prince Regent, the future George IV. In 1812 John Nash designed the park we see today as the grounds for a new palace for the future George IV.

Pocket Tip

Regent's Park Open Air Theatre *is open from May to September. You can bring a picnic and eat it under the fairy lights twinkling in the trees and choose from variety of theatrical performances such as* Lord of the Flies, The Beggar's Opera *and* Pericles, *as featured on the 2011 programme. The nearest tube stations are Regent's Park and Baker Street.*

Regent's Park is the biggest outdoor sports area in London and is used for a number of sports including football, rugby, cricket and softball. There is a multi-sports facility called 'The Hub', which provides children's activities and exercise classes and a café with 360-degree views of the park. ZSL London Zoo is also located in Regent's Park and is the world's oldest scientific zoo with over 720 species of animals.

Pocket Tip

At The Hub you can pick up a pocket-sized running routes' map, which shows some great running paths in the park.

Primrose Hill

Primrose Hill is the highest point in Regent's Park and the climb to the top is well worth it as you have fantastic views of London all the way to St Paul's Cathedral.

Pocket Tip 🖋

There are 12 city farms in London where you can see farmyard animals, gardens, children's play areas and buy farm produce. For more details, go to the Visit London website (www.visitlondon.com/attractions/outdoors/city-farms).

OTHER LONDON PARKS

Richmond Park

In the 1300s Richmond Park was originally part of the Manor of Sheen owned by Edward I and was enclosed in 1625 by Charles II. It is 2,500 acres in size and is the largest park in London with over 650 red and fallow deer roaming freely.

Hampstead Heath

The heath covers an area of 791 acres and is London's wildest park. In 1989 management of the heath was given to the City of London, which maintains the mixture of heath, woodland and ponds. From Parliament Hill there are wonderful views of London all the way to Canary Wharf and in the summer months you can swim in the lido or the bathing ponds. John Keats, the 19th-century poet, lived on the edge of the heath in Wentworth Lodge.

Bushy Park

In 1529 the park, consisting of 1,099 acres, was given to Henry VIII by Cardinal Wolsey, who created a deer chase. In 1610 Charles I started to landscape the park by creating the Longford River. There are the spectacular Upper Lodge water gardens consisting of pools, cascades, a canal and woodland gardens with winding paths and rippling streams. The red and fallow deer still roam through the park as they did during the time of Henry VIII.

Greenwich Park

This is the oldest park and covers 183 acres. In 1433 the park was enclosed by Richard, Duke of Gloucester, the brother of Henry V. In the 1660s Charles II remodelled the park in a formal design inspired by the French landscape architect André le Nôtre, the gardener of Louis XIV of France. There are wonderful views of London from the top of the hill all the way to St Paul's Cathedral. During the 2012 Olympics Greenwich Park will be the location for the equestrian events.

Royal Botanic Gardens at Kew – a World Heritage Site

Kew Gardens consists of 300 acres of the most wonderful trees and plants with elegant hot houses filled with unusual plants and orchids and a treetop walk. In the 18th century George III employed Joseph Banks to send botanical collectors around the world to collect unusual specimens. Today Kew is a research centre and has the largest plant collection in the world. The garden is home to a wild flock of bright green ring-necked parakeets, which are native to South Asia. The urban legend is that they escaped from the film set of The African Queen*! The nearest tube station is Kew Gardens and you can visit its website (www.kew.org) for more details.*

🚕 SECRET GARDENS 🚕

There are many London gardens that are open to the public but which are not as well known as the royal parks. These range from tiny but perfect little gardens in the walled ruins of bombed-out churches in the city, to the large gardens of the Royal Hospital Chelsea.

THE GARDENS, ROYAL HOSPITAL CHELSEA

This garden is 66 acres of parkland and trees that surround the Royal Hospital Chelsea. For the majority of the year this a relatively quiet place but if you add the words 'Chelsea Flower Show', suddenly there are thousands of people visiting for five days in late May. It is one of the premier garden shows and is a riot of colour with all the flowers and plants on show in marquees and gardens.

CHELSEA PHYSIC GARDEN

This secret garden was founded in 1673 by the Worshipful Society of Apothecaries of London as a place for its apprentices to study medicine. It is a herb garden and is the second oldest botanical garden in Britain. The Chelsea Physic Garden is now involved in furthering education in natural medicine and its gardens include the World and Pharmaceutical Medicine gardens. For more information, see (www.chelseaphysicgarden.co.uk).

Pocket Fact

Chelsea Physic Garden has the most northerly fruiting grape-fruit tree in the world because the riverside location is so warm.

GARDEN SQUARES

London has 600 garden squares which provide green spaces for the homes around the squares. Several are permanently open to the public such as Tavistock, Bloomsbury and Russell squares in Bloomsbury but a number of these little oases remain closed to the public and are looked after by the residents of the square. However, once a year they are open to the public, during the Open Garden Squares Weekend. For more information, see the website (www.opensquares.org).

London's best kept secrets: small gardens

- *St Dunstan in the East, St Dunstan Hill.*
- *Postman's Park, King Edward Street.*
- *Temple Gardens, between Fleet Street and Embankment.*

- *Bunhill Fields Burial Ground, City Road.*
- *Victoria Embankment Gardens, Embankment.*
- *Garden Museum, Lambeth.*
- *St Paul's Cathedral.*
- *Kyoto Japanese Garden, Holland Park.*
- *The Salters Company Garden, Fore Street.*

🚗 SPORTING EVENTS IN LONDON 🚗

A number of sporting events take place in London throughout the year, where you can watch world-class events, from tennis to cricket to rowing.

WIMBLEDON

Wimbledon Tennis Tournament takes place in June and July and is the only grand slam competition played on grass. There is something special about Wimbledon: perhaps it is the famous centre court or the traditional fare of strawberries and cream but Wimbledon remains a highlight of the sporting year in London.

Pocket Fact 🌉
During the tournament 23 tonnes of strawberries and 7,000 litres of cream are consumed.

The tournament, which is run by the Lawn Tennis Association, has taken place since 1877, with over 60 nations taking part in the five main championship events plus veterans, wheelchair and junior competitions. When the tournament is not taking place you can take a tour around its famous courts and pretend just for a moment that you are Andy Murray.

Buying tickets for Wimbledon

You can submit an application for the public ballot. Ticket prices are between £35 and £100.

Each day you can turn up to try to get one of the 500 tickets for Centre Court and the No. 2 Court for days 1–9, or one of the 500 tickets for the No. 1 court for days 1–13. There are also several thousand ground admission tickets, which allow you entry in the outside courts or to watch on the big screen within the grounds. For more details go to the Wimbledon website (www.wimbledon.com).

LONDON MARATHON

The London Marathon was first run in 1981and is the one of the few times you can see a lobster racing a tiger, a gingerbread man and a banana. It takes place annually in April and was founded by Chris Brasher and John Disley, who were inspired by the New York Marathon. They got permission to close the roads in the centre of London and were able to set up a course that is like a tour route of all the major sites, going past St Paul's Cathedral, the Tower of London, over Tower Bridge and down the Mall. The runners in the London Marathon are chosen by public ballot or you can obtain a place by applying to the charities that have guaranteed places. For more details go to marathon website (www.virginlondonmarathon.com).

Pocket Fact

In 2010, 36,000 people took part in the London Marathon. The oldest man to take part was Jerzy Kolodziej, aged 86, and the oldest women was Irene Clarke, aged 83.

LONDON 2012 OLYMPICS

London has previously hosted the games in 1908 at White City and in 1948 at Wembley Stadium, and there was huge jubilation when it was announced in 2005 that London would host the 2012 games in the East End. Part of the reason that London's bid for 2012 was successful was because of the proposal to regenerate a large derelict area around Stratford (an area of 500 acres) as the Olympic Park. After the games the Olympic Park will provide new international sporting facilities including swimming and cycling, and the Olympic stadium will be used by West Ham football club.

2012 Olympic Park facts

- The main press centre has a brown roof made up of gravel and moss to encourage wildlife.

- 30 bridges have been built to span the numerous waterways.

- 63% of the building materials were transported by rail or river.

- 650 bird and bat boxes are installed across the park including within bridges and on the roof of the main press centre.

- 438,000 plants, trees and bulbs are being planted.

- A rare community of great crested newts were relocated to a refurbished existing pond to make way for the velodrome.

Past London Olympics

The 1908 games were awarded to Rome but that city could not stage them as Mt Vesuvius erupted and so the games moved to London instead. In the 1908 games the marathon was lengthened to start from the window at Windsor Castle so that the royal children could watch the start of the race. The end was at the royal box at White City, and this distance of 26 miles and 385 yards is now the standard distance for the race.

The 1948 Olympics were the first games since 1936 because of the Second World War and because of rationing and a shortage of money came to be known as the austerity games. The 1948 games were so short of money that the athletes stayed in the old RAF barracks in Uxbridge and were given vouchers to travel on public transport to their events.

The 2012 mascots

- *The 2012 London Olympic mascots are called Wenlock and Mandeville.*
- *Wenlock was inspired by Much Wenlock in Shropshire as the games held in this small town were part of the inspiration for the modern Olympic movement.*
- *Mandeville was inspired by Stoke Mandeville, the birthplace of the Paralympics.*
- *Wenlock is silver and yellow and Mandeville is silver and blue. Both mascots have one eye representing a camera and they have taxi lights on their head inspired by London taxi cabs.*

SPORTING VENUES IN LONDON

London is home to some fantastic world-class sporting venues such as Lords' and the Oval for cricket, Twickenham stadium for rugby and Wembley stadium for football.

CRICKET: LORD'S AND KIA OVAL

Did you know: Lord's has been the headquarters of the Middlesex County Cricket Club since 1814 and is considered the home of English cricket. The Kia Oval has been the home of Surrey County Cricket Club since 1845.

Events held there: The Ashes, a biennial cricket series between Australia and England.

Pocket Fact

The Ashes series gets its name from the ashes of the bails from the match in 1882, when England lost to Australia for the first time.

RUGBY: TWICKENHAM STADIUM

Did you know: Twickenham is the home of English rugby and is the largest dedicated rugby stadium in the world, seating 82,000 people. The first game was played here in 1909.

Events held here: The annual Six Nations rugby championship between England, France, Ireland, Italy, Scotland and Wales. In the 2015 Rugby World Cup the final, semi-finals and one quarter final will be played here.

Pocket Fact 🚉

In the 2015 Rugby World Cup rugby will be played at Arsenal's football ground for the first time.

FOOTBALL: WEMBLEY STADIUM

Did you know: since 1923 Wembley has been the home of English football. The twin towers of the old stadium held a special place in the hearts of English football supporters as it was here in 1966 that England won the World Cup. The present stadium was designed by Norman Foster and was opened in 2007. It seats 90,000 people and is the second largest stadium in Europe.

Events held here: England's international matches, FA Cup semi-finals and final, Championship final, the Carling Cup and the football finals of the 2012 London Olympics.

London's football teams and their stadiums

- *Arsenal: The Emirates Stadium, Highbury.*
- *Chelsea: Stamford Bridge, Fulham.*
- *Tottenham Hotspur: White Hart Lane, Tottenham.*
- *West Ham United: Upton Park, Newham.*
- *Millwall: The Den, Bermondsey.*
- *Fulham: Craven Cottage, Fulham.*
- *Queens Park Rangers: Loftus Road, Shepherds Bush.*
- *Crystal Palace: Selhurst Park, Croydon.*
- *Charlton Athletic: The Valley, Charlton.*

🚕 THE THAMES 🚕

The river Thames is the lifeblood of London. The river provided a means of travel and drinking water for the early tribes that lived along its banks and continued to be a vital route for trade and commerce throughout the growth of the city. From the Romans until the 1980s it was a trading port and today, at Tilbury in the river estuary to the east, it is one of the three largest ports in Britain.

Today the river is used for transport, rowing, canoeing and walking along the Thames Path, where you can find some fantastic views of the city.

Pocket Tip 🖊

The Thames Path is a National Trail footpath that runs 180 miles from the Thames Barrier to Kemble in Gloucestershire. For more details on the Thames Path go to its website (www. thames-path.org.uk).

The Thames begins its journey as a little stream 210 miles away in the Cotswolds. By the time it reaches London it has become tidal which means it rises and falls as much as 21ft every day. This means there are very strong currents which makes it very dangerous to swim in. There are four RNLI (Royal National Lifeboat Institution) lifeboats stationed along the Thames. The Tower lifeboat at Waterloo Bridge is staffed by 46 volunteers and rescued 118 people in 2010.

For nearly 200 years the Thames was described as 'dead water' because it was so polluted. After a massive clean-up campaign there are now over 120 species of fish in the river; you can even fish for trout by Westminster Bridge and near Dagenham in East London a colony of rare seahorses has been found.

THE BRIDGES

The first Thames bridge was London Bridge, a wooden bridge built by the Romans. It was not until 1209 that the first stone bridge was completed under the supervision of Peter de

Colechurch. This bridge remained the only river crossing for 500 years as the City of London refused to allow another bridge to be built because it believed that trade would move away from the City. The present London Bridge was opened in 1973.

Myths & Legends 🚌

The nursery rhyme London Bridge is Falling Down *is said to refer to the destruction of the bridge by King Olaf II in 1014.*

Putney Bridge, linking Putney and Fulham, was the first crossing to be built after the city lifted the ban on building bridges. It was followed by 17 bridges built from Richmond to the Tower of London including two pedestrian bridges, the Golden Jubilee and Millennium bridges.

The best Thames bridges

- *Prettiest: Albert Bridge is lit up at night by over 400 bulbs.*
- *Most iconic: Tower Bridge with its wonderful towers.*
- *Oldest bridge: Richmond Bridge built in 1777.*
- *Best pedestrian bridge: Millennium Bridge is the newest with great views of the City of London and of St Paul's Cathedral at one end and the Tate Modern at the other.*
- *Best views: From Waterloo Bridge you can see St Paul's and the City of London as well as the Houses of Parliament and the London Eye.*

Pocket Tip 🕯

The Thames is a wonderful way to travel through London and to view the city in a different way. River buses and cruises run at regular intervals from Westminster Bridge to Greenwich or from Tate Britain to Tate Modern. For details of river transport and tours go to the Transport of London website (www. tfl.gov.uk).

BOAT RACING

The Thames is famous for its river races throughout the year. From the Oxford and Cambridge boat race to Henley Royal Regatta, the events are numerous and varied.

Oxford and Cambridge boat race

The race began in 1829 when Cambridge challenged Oxford. It is raced every year in March or April by a coxed rowing eight over a 4 mile course from Putney Bridge to Chiswick Bridge and attracts over 250,000 spectators. For more details go to the race's website (www.theboatrace.org).

Henley Royal Regatta

The event began in 1839 and was originally staged as a family attraction and included a fair. Now it is a series of 19 amateur rowing races over five days and takes place at the end of June. For more details go to its website (www.hrr.co.uk).

Doggett's coat and badge race

This race was introduced in 1715 by Thomas Doggett, who provided a red coat and a silver badge as a prize for a race between newly qualified Thames watermen (transport passengers) and lightermen (transport goods). It is raced in July from London Bridge to Chelsea, a distance of just over 4 miles in single sculls. For more details go to the race's website (www.watermenshall.org/trainings).

The great river race

This is a handicapped race over 21 miles from Millwall Riverside to Richmond, which began in 1988. The race takes place in September and features over 300 boats from all over the world, carrying around 2,000 competitors, some in fancy dress, racing for 35 trophies ranging from the overall winner to the crew that raises the most money. For more details go to its website (www.greatriverrace.co.uk).

Some famous boats moored on the Thames

- **HMS Belfast**: The 1939 Second World War Royal Navy cruiser is moored on the Thames at Tooley Street. The ship is now a museum where you can find out what life was like on board.

- **Cutty Sark**. The Cutty Sark will reopen in 2012 at Greenwich after extensive renovation after a devastating fire. Built in 1869 she is the world's last tea clipper and was the fastest ship in the race to bring the tea harvest back to London from China in the 1870s. Later in the 1880s she broke numerous records sailing from Sydney to London carrying wool.

- **Golden Hinde**. A reconstruction of the famous Tudor warship of Sir Francis Drake in which he circumnavigated the globe in 1577–1580, the ship is moored at Pickfords Wharf, Clink Street.

8

DARKER LONDON

Looking at London's modern façade today it is difficult to imagine that it was once full of dungeons, prisons, public executions, Jack the Ripper and notorious gangsters. This chapter will tell the stories of darker London that will make your blood run a little bit colder. It will describe the places where you can still get a feel for what it was like to be imprisoned or tortured, which criminal had the most notorious reputation and some of the best ghost stories in London.

TOWER OF LONDON

The Tower was used to instil terror into the hearts of the population. Whether you were Queen or commoner the Tower had a fearsome reputation for there were many ways to die within its high impenetrable walls, either by torture or execution.

Crimes that would get you imprisoned in the Tower included:

- Extortion.

- Suspicion of disloyalty.

- Treason, covering a multitude of actions against the monarchy, including adultery.

- Denouncing flogging in the army and corruption in Parliament.

- Spying.

Pocket Fact ⚓

Sir Thomas More was kept in the dungeon at the base of the Bell Tower for 14 months during which time his beard grew very long. At his execution for treason in July 1535 he asked the executioner to wait while he rolled up his beard as it had committed no treason.

BEAUCHAMP TOWER

The Beauchamp Tower is one of the 12 towers built into the inner wall that surrounds the Tower. It is situated to the west of the Scaffold site on Tower Green and was used mainly for aristocratic prisoners. Its very walls demonstrate how many prisoners were incarcerated here, as there are numerous carvings, many of them highly decorative, carved between 1532 and 1672. Some of the carvings were done by people of high status, such as Sir Philip Howard, Earl of Arundel. He was accused of high treason in 1585 by Elizabeth I, but was never tried and died after being imprisoned for 10 years.

Lady Jane Grey

The simple carving of the name 'Jane' etched into the wall of the Beauchamp Tower was possibly done by Lord Guildford Dudley, the husband of Lady Jane Grey. Jane's powerful family had insisted that she claim the throne of England despite her claim being tenuous (she was the granddaughter of Mary, the sister of Henry VIII) but she was Queen for just nine days in 1553 before she was captured by Mary I. She was imprisoned in the Tower and executed when she was just 16 years old. Lady Jane Grey's ghost has been said to have appeared a number of times on the anniversary of her execution. The best documented occasion was in 1957 when a guardsman witnessed a white shape forming into a woman on the anniversary of Lady Jane Grey's death.

BLOODY TOWER

The Bloody Tower used to be called the Garden Tower until the mysterious disappearance of the princes in the Tower. When Edward IV died in 1483, his sons, 12-year-old Edward V, the heir to the throne, and his 10-year-old brother Richard, were taken to the Tower for safe keeping by their uncle, Richard of Gloucester.

The coronation was planned for the young king but it never happened as Richard declared Edward IV's marriage invalid, making Edward V illegitimate, and instead had himself crowned King Richard III. The princes continued to be seen playing in the grounds of the Tower until they disappeared from view around 1483. In 1674, when work was being done on the White Tower, the bones of two teenage children were found and presumed to be the young princes and were buried in Westminster Abbey. The murderer was never found although many names are in the frame including Richard III, Henry Stafford, Duke of Buckingham and Henry VII.

Prisoners at the Tower of London

- The first prisoner was Ranulf Flambard in 1100, who escaped by climbing down a rope which had been smuggled inside a wine barrel.

- The last person to be imprisoned at the Tower of London was Rudolph Hess, Deputy Führer of Nazi Germany, who was held at the Queen's House from 17–21 May 1941.

- The longest serving prisoner was Sir William de la Pole, who was imprisoned for 37 years in 1502 by Henry VII. He was never released and died in prison.

TORTURE AT THE WAKEFIELD TOWER

Torture was used extensively during a relatively short period from the 16th to the 17th century mainly because of religious upheaval. However, there was some doubt as to how successful it was because if you were being stretched on the rack and wanted them to stop you would tell them whatever they wanted to know.

People were usually tortured not to make them confess but to reveal co-conspirators, safe houses and letter routes. The warders of the Tower (Beefeaters, see p.154) were responsible for carrying out the torture but often just the sight of the torture instruments would be enough to loosen the tongues of the prisoners.

Some instruments of torture used at the Tower of London

- *The rack: your arms and legs were stretched by tying them to the rollers which then turned to stretch the body until the limbs dislocated and were torn from their sockets.*
- *The manacles: you were hung from iron handcuffs around your wrists with your feet dangling off the floor. It was considered a less severe torture but the pain was extreme as your entire body weight was hung off your wrists.*
- *The scavenger's daughter: your body was compressed into a sitting position by an iron frame. The compression of the body led to bleeding from the nose and ears and if compressed even more could result in broken bones.*

THE RAVENS

The association of ravens with the Tower is not surprising as they have always been linked with dark stories, superstition and death. It is not uncommon to hear the group described as an 'unkindness of ravens' and there were certainly many unkind things going on at the Tower.

Pocket Fact 🌉

Ravens can imitate human speech and Thor, one of the ravens at the Tower, says 'good morning' and can imitate the Ravenmaster's voice when he calls the ravens for bed. The Ravenmaster is the yeoman warder responsible for the care of the ravens and they wear a badge on their arm of a raven's head encircled by a crown.

Ravens are black birds from the crow family whose infamous reputation stems from their unfortunate eating habits as they were often seen on battlefields picking at the dead bodies. It is believed that it was their fondness for carrion that first drew them to the Tower as the moat surrounding the Tower was not flushed out by the tide of the Thames so lots of 'food' was left behind for the ravens.

Pocket Fact

Some of the ravens have not stayed at the Tower. Raven George was dismissed for eating television aerials and Raven Grog was last seen outside an East End pub in 1981.

The legend of the Tower is that there must be six ravens at the Tower otherwise the Tower will crumble and the monarchy will fall. Today there are seven ravens kept at the Tower just in case one should die. Today's ravens are called:

- Thor: after the god of war.

- Hugine and Munin: named after two mythical Norse ravens.

- Bran and Branwen: from the Irish name for ravens.

- Gwyllum: from the Welsh, as ravens are native to Wales.

- Cedric: after the historic founder of Wessex.

Pocket Tip

The ravens can be seen walking around the Tower mainly on Tower Green and the green area in front of the entrance to the White Tower.

The ravens wear coloured rings on their legs for identification and have a meat-rich diet of fresh meat from Smithfield Market, rabbit, eggs and a monthly dose of cod liver oil to keep their feathers glossy. Jim Crow was the oldest raven living to 44 years old.

Myths & Legends 🚌

In the 17th century King Charles II was so concerned about the raven legend that when the royal astronomer Sir John Flamstead complained that the ravens were messing on his telescope, Charles moved him to Greenwich rather than move the ravens.

🚌 EXECUTIONS 🚌

London had a number of execution sites which included Tower Green inside the Tower of London, Tower Hill, Smithfield, Tyburn and Newgate. All of these sites were host to some grisly scenes and form a darker part of London's history.

TOWER GREEN AND TOWER HILL

Tower Green was used for the nobility because they had earned the right to be executed in private within the Tower walls. It was also used if the authorities thought that a public execution would be unpopular, as in the case of the Earl of Essex who had plotted a revolt against Queen Elizabeth I.

Those executed on Tower Green

- *1483, William Lord Hastings: beheaded for supporting the young Edward V.*
- *1536, Anne Boleyn, second wife of Henry VIII: beheaded for adultery.*
- *1542, Catherine Howard, fifth wife of Henry VIII: beheaded for adultery.*
- *1542, Jane, Viscountess Rochford, lady-in-waiting to Catherine Howard: beheaded for keeping Catherine Howard's adultery a secret.*
- *1554, Lady Jane Grey: beheaded for trying to claim the throne from Mary Tudor.*
- *1743, Farquar Shaw, Samuel and Malcolm MacPherson: soldiers of the Scottish regiment the Black Watch who were shot for deserting their post.*

On Tower Hill, just outside the Tower of London, the public executions were like a football match as thousands of unruly spectators would turn out to watch. Around 36 beheadings took place there from 1381 to 1747. The last execution to take place was that of Lord Lovat in 1745 who was executed for his part in trying to restore Bonnie Prince Charlie as king.

Myths & Legends

The handsome and popular illegitimate son of Charles II, the Duke of Monmouth was beheaded in 1685 for attempting to take the throne from his uncle James II. It was common practice for the condemned person to pay the executioner and it is said that the duke did not pay the executioner which is why it took five blows to chop his head off.

SMITHFIELD

Smithfield was used for public gatherings including tournaments, fairs and that other favourite spectator sport, executions. Smithfield is where the commoners were executed, mainly by burning for being heretics, witches and traitors. In 1305 one of the most notable executions took place here, that of the Scottish rebel William Wallace, who led a rebellion against King Edward I to free Scotland from English rule. He was captured and executed at Smithfield and a plaque on the wall commemorates his death.

Pocket Fact

William Wallace was subjected to the ultimate punishment of being hanged, drawn and quartered. He was dragged through the streets of London to Smithfield. Hanged until not quite dead, he was then drawn (disembowelled), and quartered (head chopped off and body cut into quarters) and his head placed on a spike on London Bridge.

Boiling in oil was another means of execution used at this time, normally reserved for coin forgers and poisoners. After the 16th-century executions at Smithfield were stopped as Tyburn became the main execution site.

TYBURN

In 1196 the first recorded hanging took place at Tyburn, which was situated where Marble Arch stands today. As more and more crimes became capital offences a more efficient way was needed to dispatch the condemned, so in 1571 a gallows was built called the Tyburn Tree or Triple Tree which could hang up to 24 people in one go.

Crimes punishable by death

In the 18th century over 200 crimes were punishable by death, which included:

- *Cutting down a tree.*
- *Stealing horses or sheep.*
- *Destroying turnpike roads.*
- *Pickpocketing goods worth more than 1 shilling.*
- *Being out at night with a blackened face.*
- *Arson.*
- *Forgery.*
- *Stealing from a rabbit warren.*
- *Murder.*

Most of the prisoners were brought from Newgate Prison in the City of London. On the Sunday prior to their execution a hand bell would be rung at midnight outside their cell and the following morning the bell would be rung at the church of St Sepulchre without Newgate to let people know that it was an execution day.

Prisoners would travel through the streets for 3 miles on the back of carts from Newgate Prison to Tyburn (Marble Arch) often sitting on their coffins. There would be huge crowds, some throwing things or shouting or hanging out of the windows to get a good view of the condemned, especially if it was somebody notorious.

Myths & Legends 🚌

The term 'on the wagon' is used to describe someone who is not drinking. It is unclear whether the phrase stems from the prisoners, who after having their customary drink en route to Tyburn, would be put back on the wagon never to drink again, or to the executioner who was not allowed to get off to have a drink, but the origins are grisly nonetheless!

The Monday hangings attracted huge crowds of up to 100,000 and it was a real party atmosphere with street vendors selling food and souvenirs. Once the executions had taken place it was bedlam as people fought to touch the dead, believing that their touch could cure many different illnesses.

In 1783 the last hanging to take place was of highwayman John Austin. The public hangings then moved to Newgate, not because of any squeamishness at thousands of people watching multiple hangings, but because the crowds were becoming so large and rowdy that the rich people who had moved into Oxford Street and Mayfair, the areas around Tyburn, did not like all the noise and mess.

NEWGATE AND THE OLD BAILEY

When the hangings moved from Tyburn to Newgate (now the site of the Central Criminal Courts, commonly known as the Old Bailey) it was no longer necessary to drag the prisoners through London for their execution.

There had been a prison at Newgate since the 12th century, and by the 18th century Newgate was the largest and most notorious of the 150 prisons in London. Your life in the prison depended on your ability to pay for food, candles, soap, a bed, freedom to walk around or a visiting lady of ill repute, so if you were poor your life inside was abject misery. The area around Newgate was much smaller but this did not prevent crowds of sometimes 30,000 from watching the executions.

Pocket Fact 🌉

Charles Dickens was one of the many people disgusted by public executions and in 1849 wrote to The Times *to complain about 'the indecent spectacle of public executions'. Dickens describes Newgate on the day of an execution in his novel* Oliver Twist.

With so many people crammed into such a small area it was often as dangerous for the spectator as the condemned, as many people were trampled underfoot in the large crowds. In 1868 the last public hangings took place and further executions were carried out within the walls of Newgate Prison. Today this dark part of London's history may seem a long time ago, but to put this in perspective by the time the last public hanging took place you could travel on the new underground railway from Paddington Station to Farringdon Street via King's Cross.

The last execution in London took place at Pentonville prison on 6 July 1961. In 1965 the death penalty was abolished for murder but you could still be executed for high treason, 'piracy with violence' (piracy with intent to kill or cause grievous bodily harm), arson in royal dockyards and espionage. It was not until 1998 that the death penalty was completely abolished.

Executioner's dock

The execution of pirates was carried out at Wapping where those convicted of piracy were hanged from a scaffold erected at low tide on a short rope which meant that they did not die immediately but danced the 'Marshal's Dance' on the end of the rope. They were then left for three tides before being cut down. The last execution here was in 1830.

🚗 FAMOUS CRIMES AND CRIMINALS 🚗

In a large city like London there have been a number of notorious crimes and criminals, some of them with fearsome reputations, such as Jack the Ripper and the Kray twins, who today have become part of London's legends.

JACK THE RIPPER

The identity of Jack the Ripper has remained shrouded in myth and mystery, mainly because he was never captured. In the 1880s the area around Whitechapel was notorious for its poverty, petty crime and prostitution. During the period from 3 April 1888 to 13 April 1891, 11 women were murdered and these crimes became known as the 'Whitechapel Murders'. There are varying accounts of how many of these murders could be attributed to Jack the Ripper but the consensus is that five of the murders were carried out by the same man because of the similarities between the murders.

Jack the Ripper's five victims

- *31 August 1888, Mary Ann (Polly) Nichols: found in Buck's Row (now Durward Street) with her throat slit and her abdomen cut open.*
- *8 September 1888, Annie Chapman: found in Hanbury Street with the same injuries as Nichols.*
- *30 September 1888, Lizzie Stride: found in what is now Henriques Street with her throat cut. It is thought that the murderer was disturbed before he could continue.*
- *30 September 1888, Cathy Eddowes: found in Mitre Square 15 minutes after Lizzie Stride with her throat slit and abdomen cut open.*
- *9 November 1888, Mary Jane Kelly: found in her room in Dorset Square with her throat cut and her body badly mutilated.*

The police named the killer 'Jack the Ripper', but this was incorrect as judging by his skill with a knife he could have been a surgeon or butcher.

Pocket Fact 🌉

The name 'Jack the Ripper' was taken from a letter supposedly sent by the murderer to the Central News Agency and signed Jack the Ripper.

Jack the Ripper has continued to fire people's imaginations today, as the subject of walking tours, films, television programmes and books. His story fascinates people just as it did then as speculation continues as to who the murderer may have been. The theories run from the Duke of Clarence, the grandson of Queen Victoria, to Aaron Kominski, a member of London's Polish Jewish population, Thomas Cutbush, the nephew of a Scotland Yard superintendent, and Montague John Druitt, a prominent local physician whose body was found floating in the river Thames in December 1888, possibly explaining the sudden end to the murders.

Pocket Tip ❗

For information on Jack the Ripper walks around the area of Whitechapel where the murders took place go to the Blue Badge guide website or London walks website (www.blue-badge-guides.com or www.walks.com). The Ten Bells pub, where the victims drank, is still to be found on the corner of Commercial Street and Fournier Street.

THE KRAY TWINS

The Kray twins, Ronnie and Reggie, were notorious gangsters in the 1960s who controlled a number of pubs and clubs and were involved in murder, armed robberies, violent assaults and protection rackets. In London's East End they were considered by some to be heroes as they 'looked after their own', were good to their mum and appeared to be working-class lads who had 'done all right for themselves'.

Myths & Legends 🚃

The rumour goes that the Kray twins disposed of a body in one of the supporting pillars of the M6 when it was being built.

When the Krays started to open clubs in the West End they became part of the 'Swinging London' scene. In 1960 Reggie was given Esmeralda's Barn, a nightclub in Knightsbridge by Peter Rachman, the head of a violent landlord operation. This club became very popular with celebrities and the twins now had two lives, that of violent gangsters and celebrity nightclub owners, where they mixed with a number famous celebrities and were photographed by David Bailey, with guests including:

- Frank Sinatra

- Barbara Windsor

- Francis Bacon

- George Raft

- Judy Garland.

In 1968 Ronnie and Reggie Kray and 18 members of their gang were arrested during a dawn raid in London. They were eventually convicted at the Old Bailey for the murders of George Cornell and Jack 'The Hat' McVitie and given life imprisonment. There were several unsuccessful campaigns to get them released and eventually Ronnie died of a heart attack in prison in 1995 while Reggie died from cancer in 2000, after having been released on compassionate grounds.

OTHER NOTORIOUS LONDON MURDERS

1785: Sweeney Todd

The demon barber of Fleet Street supposedly murdered his clients and then baked their flesh in meat pies helped by his girl-friend/accomplice.

1811: Ratcliff murders

The Ratcliff murders were the mysterious murders of two families, Timothy Marr, his wife, son, shop worker and servant on 7 December 1811 and John Williamson, his wife and servant on 19 December 1811.

1940s and 1950s: 10 Rillington Place murder

Reginald Christie murdered six women. His lodger Timothy Evans was hanged for the murder of his wife and child and in 1965 an enquiry established that they were murdered by Christie.

1940s: John George Haigh

Haigh murdered six people whose bodies he disposed of in acid.

1970s and 1980: Dennis Nilsen

Nilsen lived in Cricklewood and Muswell Hill and murdered at least 15 men and boys.

1974: Lord Lucan

He allegedly murdered the family nanny and disappeared.

🚗 GHOSTS AND THINGS THAT 🚗 GO BUMP IN THE NIGHT

When you read about all the terrible things that happened to people in London it doesn't seem so strange that London has a huge number of ghost stories. From executed queens to sisters looking for their dead brother there are a multitude of ghost stories based in the city.

Anne Boleyn and the Tower of London

Anne Boleyn is the ghost most frequently seen at the Tower of London. Several people have reported seeing her headless body leading a procession of lords and ladies down the aisle of St Peter Vincula, the church inside the Tower where she is buried.

Cleopatra's Needle, Embankment

This section of the river has always been popular with suicides and one story tells of a tall naked figure that jumps into the river and while no splash is heard there is strange laughter.

Adelphi Theatre, Strand

In 1897 actor-manager William Terris was stabbed to death outside the stage door by a fellow actor. His presence has been sensed in the theatre and the tapping of his stick has been heard on several occasions. He is also said to haunt Covent Garden tube station where a tall man in a frock coat has been seen. The station is on the site of a baker's shop that Terris used to visit.

St James's Park

Several people, including members of the Coldstream Guards who guard the royal palaces, have seen a headless woman in a red striped dress either emerging from the lake or walking across the park. She was first seen in the early 1800s and again as recently as 1972. She is said to be the murdered wife of a soldier at the barracks who had chopped his wife's head off and was just about to throw her in the lake when he was discovered.

St Thomas's hospital

Florence Nightingale is supposed to haunt the hospital where she had her nursing school. A ghost dressed in a pre-1920 nurse's uniform is often seen by patients and nurses. She can only be seen from the calf up as the level of the floor was raised.

The Bank of England

In 1811 Philip Whitehead who worked at the Bank of England was found guilty of forgery and hanged. When his sister Sarah found out what had happened to him, she went mad and continued to turn up at the bank every day asking for him. Even after her death several people have been stopped by a ghostly figure who asks them, 'Have you seen my brother?'.

Cemeteries in London worth a visit

- **Highgate**. *Opened in 1839 this Victorian cemetery is a leafy oasis and contains many famous graves, including those of the authors Douglas Adams, Beryl Bainbridge and George Eliot (Mary Ann Cross), as well as the parents of Charles Dickens, the artist William Michael Rossetti, the scientist Michael Faraday and, the most famous occupant, Karl Marx. There are guided tours of the cemetery. For information go to the cemetery website (www. highgate-cemetery.org/index.php/tours).*

- **Kensal Green**. *This is one London's oldest cemeteries, which opened in 1833 and is in the heart of London between Kensington and Chelsea and Hammersmith and Fulham. The 75 acre site is managed as a nature reserve and has over 33 different species of birds. Over 500 members of the aristocracy are buried here including a son of George III, the writers Wilkie Collins, William Makepeace Thackeray and Anthony Trollope and the engineer Isambard Kingdom Brunel. For information on guided tours of the cemetery see Richard Jones's London Walking Tours website (www.walksoflondon.co.uk/36/index.shtml).*

- **Bunhill Fields**. *Located in the City, Bunhill Fields dates from 1665 when it was used as a burial ground for plague victims. It is also a former burial ground for dissenters. The most elaborate tomb is that of John Bunyan, who died in 1689. Other notable occupants include the writers William Blake and Daniel Defoe and the founder of the Quakers, George Fox.*

9

LONDON ICONS

When you think of London there are so many images that immediately pop into your head. From the famous Beefeaters to the red telephone boxes, London has a wide variety of icons which are associated with this great city. This chapter will guide you through the history and origins of some of the most famous London icons including how policemen got the nickname 'Bobby', why the yeoman warders at the Tower of London are called 'Beefeaters' and the meaning of 'apples and pears'.

🚗 LONDON'S ICONIC UNIFORMS 🚗

A lot of London's icons have become symbolic of London as a result of their characteristic uniforms. The Royal Guards, Beefeaters and even the police in London have all come to symbolise the city through both their role and their distinctive dress.

THE GUARDS

The Household Division which guards the Queen consists of the five Footguards regiments and the two regiments of the Household Cavalry. You can see these guards outside Buckingham Palace dressed in their distinctive red uniforms with their black bearskin hats. The guards are responsible for guarding Buckingham Palace, St James's Palace and the Tower of London. The total number of guards inside the palace is 36 plus three officers. When the Queen is in residence there are four guards outside in the sentry boxes and only two if she is not.

There are five Regiments of Footguards:

- Grenadier Guards (formed in 1656).

- Coldstream Guards (formed by Oliver Cromwell in 1650).

- Scots Guards (formed in 1642).

- Irish Guards (formed in 1900).

- Welsh Guards (formed in 1915).

Although they are seen carrying out ceremonial duties they are first and foremost infantry divisions deployed around the world.

Pocket Fact

The guards are allowed to march up and down but if they are standing to attention they are not allowed to move. The sentry boxes were moved inside the palace railings in 1959 because visitors were constantly tormenting them. One tourist even put a match between the fingers of the guard on duty and lit it and he still did not move.

You can tell the difference between the Guards regiments by looking at their uniforms and hats:

- Grenadier Guards: single buttons and white plume on left-side of hat.

- Coldstream Guards: buttons in pairs and red plume on right-side of hat.

- Scots Guards: buttons in threes and no plume.

- Irish Guards: buttons in fours and blue plume on right-side of hat.

- Welsh Guards: buttons in fives and white and green plume on left-side of hat.

Pocket Fact

The bearskin hats were worn in battle so that the soldiers appeared more intimidating. They are made from Canadian bearskin and some are over 100 years old.

HOUSEHOLD CAVALRY

The Household Cavalry Mounted Regiment forms the personal bodyguard of the monarch and guards the official entrance to St James's Palace in Whitehall and Buckingham Palace. It consists of the Blues and Royals, a regiment that was part of Oliver Cromwell's army in 1650, and the Life Guards, which was founded by Charles II in 1651.

Pocket Fact

Prince William, Prince Harry and the singer James Blunt have all served with the Household Cavalry.

Guards can choose to spend two years doing ceremonial duties or operational duties in the Household Cavalry regiment. They are incredibly distinctive in their uniforms with the shiny metal helmet and cuirasses (breastplate), long white gloves and extremely shiny long black boots.

Household Cavalry Facts

- *Life Guards wear red tunics and have white plumes on their helmets.*
- *Blues and Royals wear blue tunics and have red plumes on their helmets.*
- *It can take up to six hours to clean their uniform and the horses' tack.*
- *The horses are specially bred in Ireland and are always black.*
- *Each new intake of horses is known by a letter like a car registration, so if the letter was G then the horses would have names such as Gunpowder, Ghurka and Geronimo.*

BEEFEATERS

The correct name for the Beefeaters at the Tower of London is 'Yeoman Warder of Her Majesty's Royal Palace and Fortress the Tower of London, and Members of the Sovereign's Body Guard of the Yeoman Guard Extraordinary', phew! The oath of allegiance they swear on becoming a yeoman warder dates from 1337 and the role dates back to the original gaolers who guarded the prisoners.

Myths & Legends 🚌

The name 'Beefeater' is thought to come either from the fact they were given a meat ration as part of their pay or because they could eat as much beef from the king's table as they wanted.

Today their role is to guard the Tower of London, look after the ravens and the Crown Jewels, and to give extremely entertaining tours of the Tower, which begin at the main entrance every 30 minutes. They also attend the coronation, the Lord Mayor's Show and other state and charity functions.

There are 36 ordinary warders plus:

- A chief yeoman warder, who is the senior warder and is responsible for supervising the Ceremony of the Keys.

- A yeoman gaoler, who used to be responsible for prisoners but today is second in command to the chief yeoman warder.

- A Ravenmaster, who is responsible for the care of the ravens.

Pocket Tip 🖊

The 'Ceremony of the Keys' takes place every night at the Tower of London at 10pm and is the ceremonial closing of the Tower. It has been carried out by the yeoman warders for 700 years. It is free to attend this but you must apply in writing. For more details go to the website (www.hrp.org.uk/toweroflondon/whatson/ceremonyofthekeys.aspx).

To become a yeoman warder candidates must have served either in the Royal Air Force, the army or Royal Marines for 22 years, attained the rank of warrant officer and have been awarded the Good Conduct Medal. For the first time in history there is now a woman yeoman warder, appointed in 2007. The yeoman warders all live inside the Tower of London with their families and have their own chaplain, doctor and pub as the Tower is locked up at 10pm.

Uniform facts of the Beefeaters

- *Everyday wear is a blue and red uniform.*
- *The red and gold uniform with white ruff, stockings and black patent shoes is only worn on ceremonial occasions.*
- *The uniform is Tudor in style and dates from 1552. The hat is known as a Tudor bonnet.*

CITY OF LONDON POLICE AND METROPOLITAN POLICE

The first reference to policing in the City of London dates from 1252 when the term 'constable' was used, and in 1285 the Statute of Winchester set down basic obligations for the 'preservation of peace'. As London expanded in the 18th and 19th centuries, due to rising crime numbers it became obvious that London needed an organised police force. In 1828 Robert Peel set up a committee to investigate the situation and this led to the formation of the Metropolitan police.

The City of London police is responsible for one of the world's leading financial centres. In 2006 the Attorney General recommended that this police force should become the lead force for fraud and so its economic crime directorate includes the Cheque and Credit Card Unit, the Money Laundering Investigation Unit, the Fraud Intelligence Development Team and the Overseas Corruption Unit.

Pocket Fact

The police are called 'Bobbies' or 'Peelers' after Robert Peel. They are also known as the 'Old Bill' and there are over 13 reasons on the Metropolitan police website as to why they are called this, including the registration plates, BYL, used by the original vehicles of the Flying Squad (a team of detectives with specialist surveillance and firearms capabilities).

ICONIC MEANS OF TRANSPORT

Just as when you see a yellow cab you immediately think of New York, the sight of the distinctive red buses, black cabs and underground signs brings London to mind. These means of transport have all become symbols of the city.

THE LONDON BUS

One of London's most distinctive emblems is the red Routemaster bus, which was introduced in 1956. The first design had 64 seats and was 27ft 6in long and for its size was surprisingly light to drive as it had an aluminium body, power assisted steering and an automatic gearbox. It was also much more comfortable to travel in due to better suspension, and it was hoped that this would encourage more people out of their cars and on to the buses.

Pocket Fact

The Routemaster was first exhibited at the Earls Court Commercial Motor Show in 1954.

The larger RML Routemaster was introduced in 1965 with an increased length of 30ft and now carried 72 passengers. The buses operated all over London and had a driver and conductor because it was illegal to have only one operator on the bus. This was to prevent queuing at the bus stop while everyone paid on entry.

Pocket Fact ⚓

The conductors would stop people getting on if the bus was full and shout the stops out before you got to them. You were even allowed to smoke on the top deck!

The Routemaster had an open platform at the back of the bus where you boarded and got off the bus. This feature became a significant part of their iconic status and gave us the term 'hop on and hop off'. You did not have to pay as you got on because the conductor who stood in the stairwell would walk around the bus to issue paper tickets from a heavy metal machine carried on a strap around the neck. The price of the ticket was based on the length of the journey.

In 1982 the double-decker London bus started to change as the Routemaster was gradually withdrawn and single operator buses were introduced. Despite their withdrawal, the old Routemasters have retained their iconic status and for those who remember hanging off the back of the old Routemasters as children they bring back fond memories.

Routemaster buses are still used on heritage routes: the No. 15 runs from the Tower of London to Trafalgar Square and the No. 9 from the Albert Hall to Aldwych. They run from 9.30am to 6.30pm every 15 minutes, seven days a week and standard bus fares apply.

Pocket Fact ⚓

The London red bus still retains its iconic status. In 2008 when the handover of the Olympic flag from Beijing to London took place it was the red London bus that took centre stage as the iconic representative of the city.

LONDON UNDERGROUND

London Underground, or as it is more typically known 'the tube', is the oldest underground railway in the world. In 1863 the first section 'the Metropolitan', measuring nearly 4 miles, opened between Paddington (Bishop's Road) and Farringdon Street using steam locomotives.

Pocket Fact 🌉

The early steam trains needed ventilation shafts to expel the steam and bring fresh air. One of these was covered by a fake façade matching that of the houses at 23/24 Leinster Gardens, W2, to preserve the uniformity of the street. You can still see this façade today.

At first the 'cut and cover method' was used to dig the tunnels, which meant the trench was dug, the equipment laid in it and then covered over. Within a few years the Metropolitan line extended out to Buckinghamshire and the District, East London and Hammersmith and City lines were built.

The cut and cover tunnelling method was abandoned in the 19th century as it caused too much disruption. The first true 'tube' line was the City & South London Railway, opened in 1890. It was also the first electrified line on the network. The line was dug using a tunnelling shield that provided a temporary support structure while the tunnel was dug by hand.

At first all of the underground lines were operated by private companies, meaning passengers had to walk between stations to change lines. This is also the reason for the 40 unused or 'ghost' stations on the underground. Because the lines were built by the private companies, stations were built to service their own lines, even if there was already a station in that area. In 1933 when the London Passenger Transport Board (later London Transport) integrated the lines they closed some of the duplicate stations resulting in the abandoned ghost stations, such as Down Street on the Piccadilly line between Hyde Park Corner and Green Park.

Pocket Fact 🔺

In 1908 the tube's world-famous logo, 'the roundel' (a red circle crossed by a horizontal blue bar) first appeared.

The Northern line was opened in 1890 followed by Waterloo & City, Central, Bakerloo, Piccadilly and Charing Cross, Euston and Hampstead (now the Charing Cross branch of the Northern). The last lines to be built were the Victoria line, completed in 1968, and the Jubilee line, which was completed in 2000.

Top ten tube facts

- The network is 249 miles long.

- It carries 1,065 million passengers a year.

- The tube map is based on an electrical wiring diagram and was designed by Harry Beck in 1931.

- The distance travelled by the trains each year is the equivalent of 90 trips to the moon and back.

- The deepest station is Hampstead, which is 192ft below ground level.

- Amersham station is the furthest from central London at a distance of 27 miles.

- The first escalator was introduced at Earls Court station in 1911.

- Angel station has the longest escalator in western Europe at 197ft, climbing 90ft with 318 steps.

- The busiest station is Victoria, with 77 million passengers per year.

- Roding Valley is the quietest station, with just 210,000 passengers each year.

- William Gladstone and Dr Barnardo both had their coffins transported by tube.

Pocket Tip 🖋

Here are a couple of points to remember when travelling on the tube to avoid the wrath of London commuters:

- *When travelling on the escalators stand on the right unless you are walking up or down.*
- *Never, ever stop on the end of the escalator as it drives Londoners mad!*

BLACK CABS

There are 21,000 licensed taxis in London providing three million trips in and around the capital every week. But the history of the London taxi goes back to the horse-drawn hackney cabs in the 17th century. In the 19th century when the drivers began to use a lighter coach called a 'cabriolet' they were then referred to as 'cabs'. The cabs roamed the streets plying for hire and became so numerous that they had to be licensed. In 1661 the total was set at 400, in 1694 it was 700, in 1710 it was 800 and by 1850 there were 4,000 licences. From the middle of the 19th century two kinds of cabs dominated, the two-wheeled elegant hansom cab and the growler, which could carry luggage.

In 1903 the first version of the petrol-driven taxi was introduced and although it now looks a little old fashioned it is very recognisable as a London taxi. In 1906 licensing was introduced by the Public Carriage Office and despite these taxis being motorised, the licence was and still is referred to as a 'hackney carriage licence'. The term 'hackney' comes from the Arabic word 'jaca' pronounced 'haca' meaning 'a horse with a steady pace'. The word was corrupted by many languages and ended up in English as 'hackney', referring to the horse that pulled the carriage.

Pocket Fact 🚠

One of the early regulations still in place is that the taxi has to have a 25ft turning circle so they can turn around in one motion on London's crowded streets. This is why the design of the taxi has hardly changed.

Unusual laws for London taxis

- They are only allowed to accept a fare when stationary. The police allow them to flout this law though and you are allowed to hail a cab providing its yellow 'for hire' light is on.

- The driver must ask of all passengers if they have the plague.

- They are not allowed to carry a dead body or rabid dogs.

- Until 1976 they were required to carry a bale of hay to feed their horses.

Cabbie canteens

In 1875 the Earl of Shaftesbury and some friends set up the Cabmen's Shelter Fund (CSF) to provide food and shelter for horse-drawn cab drivers and to prevent them drinking on the job. Thirteen of these small green shelters are still in use providing a 'bacon sarnie' and cup of tea, and they can seat up to 13 drivers. Gambling and swearing are not allowed and the huts are now Grade II listed buildings, still run by the CSF. Go to the BBC London Cabbies' Shelters webpage (www.bbc.co.uk/dna/h2g2/ A52007041) for details of their locations, but you can only look from the outside as only cabbies can go inside!

The Knowledge

London taxi drivers are said to be the best in the world because of their extensive training, known as 'The Knowledge'. For a central London taxi, the driver has to have a detailed knowledge of an area within a 6-mile radius of Charing Cross station.

'The Knowledge' includes 25,000 roads and streets, 320 runs or routes as well as places of interest, tourist attractions and important landmarks. On average it takes 40 months to learn and pass the required tests. You can often see them training as they travel around the city on motor scooters with clipboards on their handle bars. A typical question would be to list all the theatres, streets and traffic signals on Shaftsbury Avenue.

Blue plaques

The round blue plaques started in 1866 and are placed on the outside of buildings where notable figures of the past lived and worked. There are 850 plaques in London including those of:

- *Vincent Van Gogh in Stockwell.*
- *Jimi Hendrix in Bruton Street.*
- *Karl Marx in Dean Street.*
- *Oscar Wilde in Tite Street.*
- *Wolfgang Amadeus Mozart in Ebury Street.*
- *Virginia Woolf in Fitzroy Square.*
- *Florence Nightingale in South Street.*

For more details go to the English Heritage website (www.english-heritage.org.uk/discover/blue-plaques/about/).

🚗 ICONIC LANDMARKS 🚗

London has a number of iconic landmarks that are instantly recognisable and are often used in film and television locations as an indication that the action will be taking place in London.

Big Ben

Big Ben is the famous bell which now gives its name to the clock and tower built as part of the Houses of Parliament. The clock chimed for the first time in 1859 and the bell which strikes the number of hours, weighs over 13 tonnes, the weight of a small elephant. The best view of Big Ben is at night when the dial is illuminated. See p.25 for more on Big Ben.

Nelson's column

Built in 1830 to celebrate Nelson's victory at the Battle of Trafalgar in 1805, the18ft statue of Admiral Lord Nelson stands on the top of an elegant column. When measured in 2006 the column, including Nelson, was found to be 169ft and not 185ft as everyone thought. The column stands surrounded by four lions on the edge of Trafalgar Square with its beautiful fountains.

Eros

This small statue in Piccadilly Circus was unveiled in 1893 as a memorial to the great philanthropist the Earl of Shaftesbury and was intended to be the angel of Christian charity, but is commonly known as Eros, after the Greek god of love.

Pocket Fact

The advertising around Piccadilly Circus is illuminated because in the early 1900s the local authority prevented printed advertising boards but could not prevent illuminated advertising.

Red telephone boxes

In 1923 the General Post Office launched a competition for the design of a new public telephone box. In 1926 the renowned architect Giles Gilbert Scott (who had designed Bankside Power Station, now Tate Modern) won the competition.

Pocket Fact

Gilbert Scott's design of the domed roof of the phone box was influenced by the dome on the mausoleum of Sir John Soane (the architect and famous collector) in Old St Pancras churchyard. The original wooden prototype is under the archway of the Royal Academy, Piccadilly.

This winning design, known as K2, was very expensive to produce so Gilbert Scott was asked to design K3, a much simpler model made of cast iron instead of concrete. K3 was produced in its thousands, K4 and K5 followed, and eventually K6 in 1936 which is the shape we know today. There around 946 red telephone boxes still left in London and a number of these are protected and designated Grade II listed, meaning they are of significant architectural importance.

THE LONDON EYE

The London Eye is the huge observation wheel on the south bank of the river Thames by Westminster Bridge giving incredible views over London. In 1993 the husband-and-wife architect team of Julia Barfield and David Marks designed the wheel on their kitchen table in South London. It was from these humble beginnings that the Eye was completed in time for the millennium.

In 2005 the South Bank served notice to quit on the London Eye or pay an increased rent from £64,000 to £2.5 million. The Mayor of London at the time, Ken Livingstone, intervened and threatened to issue a compulsory purchase order on the land and eventually a 25-year lease was agreed.

Interesting facts about the London Eye

- It took seven years to build and was floated down the river in sections.

- On a clear day you can see for 25 miles to Windsor Castle.

- It is one of London's most popular tourist attractions with over 2.4 million passengers a year.

- One revolution takes 30 minutes and is called a flight because the Eye was originally partly owned by British Airways.

- It has 32 capsules, which can be individually lit in different colours.

- The New Year's Eve fireworks are launched from the London Eye and because of its height the display can be seen for miles.

Paddington Bear

Paddington Bear is the star of a very popular series of children's stories written by Michael Bond about a small teddy bear from deepest darkest Peru, dressed in a blue duffel coat, red hat and red wellington boots. He was found by the Brown family on Paddington station with a label which said 'Please look after this bear. Thank you'. In the stories he is always getting into trouble and loves marmalade sandwiches. There is a statue of him at Paddington station and a cuddly version is available in a number of different costumes, including that of a Beefeater, making him a popular present for children visiting London.

🚕 COCKNEY: A TRUE LONDONER 🚕

The description of a person as 'a Cockney' was first used in 1660 and referred to a person who was born within the sound of Bow Bells, the bells of St-Mary-le-Bow in Cheapside. The sound of the bells was said to travel as far as the East End where people spoke with a distinctive London accent and used a vocabulary known as Cockney rhyming slang. Rhyming phrases were used to replace actual words so that the traders could speak among themselves without their customers or the authorities understanding them.

TEN POPULAR COCKNEY RHYMES

- Apples and pears = stairs.
- Skin and blister = sister.
- Loaf of bread = head.
- Rub-a-dub = pub.
- Butcher's hook = look.
- Ruby Murray = curry.
- Trouble and strife = wife.

- Barnet fair = hair.

- Adam and Eve = believe.

- Mother Hubbard = cupboard.

Cockney rhyming slang is still in use today but is termed 'Modern rhyming slang' with rhymes including:

- Tony Blair(s) = flares or hair.

- Ayrton Senna = tenner (£10 note).

- à la mode = code.

PEARLY KINGS AND QUEENS

The Pearly Kings and Queens originated from London's street traders who used Cockney rhyming slang. These traders date from the 11th century and were unlicensed and itinerant, selling their goods from trays and stalls, and were known as 'costermongers'. As London grew each borough elected a 'king costermonger' and 'queen costermonger' to fight for their rights.

In 1880 Henry Croft, a road sweeper and rat-catcher, was so impressed by how the costermongers helped each other during hard times that he took the fashion they had of sewing pearl buttons on the seams of their trousers, waistcoats and caps and covered an entire dress suit and top hat in elaborate patterns of pearl buttons.

Pocket Fact 🦺

There are two kinds of suits worn by Pearly Kings and Queens today; the 'smother' suit where the suit is completely covered in buttons and the 'skeleton' which has fewer buttons. The suits can weigh up to 30kg.

Croft joined the costermongers on their hospital fund raising parades and carnivals dressed in his eye-catching suit. Eventually the costermonger kings and queens adopted his idea as it was popular with the public and attracted more money for their charities. The Pearly Kings and Queens continue their charity work today, raising sums in the millions for charities such as Marie Curie, Diabetes UK, Macmillan Nurses and NSPCC.

Pocket Fact

Henry Croft died in 1930 aged 68 and his funeral was attended by around 400 'Pearlies'. He is buried in Finchley Cemetery and there is statue of him paid for by the charities that he helped in the crypt of St Martin-in-the-Fields, Trafalgar Square.

10

FOODIE LONDON

About 20–30 years ago London was considered a laughing stock when it came to good food but since then its reputation has completely changed. Now you can find a wide range of food, from traditional pie and mash and afternoon tea, to whatever national food takes your fancy. There are Lebanese, Japanese, French, Moroccan and Spanish restaurants and some of the best Indian dishes you could wish to eat. In London's shops and markets you can buy a wide range of high-quality fresh food from all over the world. This chapter will provide the background to London's famous food markets, shops and restaurants and will explore the dishes that have originated in London.

🚗 LONDON'S FOOD MARKETS 🚗

There are a number of food markets in London selling a wide variety of produce. Some of the markets are dedicated to specific produce, while others are general food markets or even ethnic markets selling a wide selection of international delicacies.

BILLINGSGATE WHOLESALE FISH MARKET

The Billingsgate fish market can trace its history back to 1699 when an act of parliament was passed to make it 'a free and open market for all sorts of fish whatsoever', except for the sale of eels. The trade in eels was the exclusive right of Dutch fishermen as they had helped feed the city during the Great Fire of London in 1660.

Pocket Fact ⊣▐⊢

The actor Michael Caine is the son of a former Billingsgate fish porter and briefly worked there before he became an actor.

In 1873 a new market designed by Horace Jones (the designer of Tower Bridge) was built to replace the old market. The building is set on the Thames river bank with wide glass doors and decorated with a large fish weather vane and fish cast into the metalwork over the windows, and is now an events space. In 1982 the market moved again and the new market, in the shadow of Canary Wharf, is the largest inland fish market in Britain. It sells on average 25,000 tonnes of fish and fish products each year. The annual turnover of the market is in the region of £200 million and it sells to shops, restaurants and hotels.

Getting to Billingsgate

- *Opening times are Tuesday to Saturday, 5am–8.30am and it is open to wholesalers and the public.*
- *The market offers training courses in preparing and cooking fish. For more details go to their website (www.seafoodtraining.org).*
- *Billingsgate does not offer regular tours of the market but if you contact them, they may be able to arrange something for you. For more information go to the City of London's tours webpage (www.cityoflondon.gov.uk/Corporation/ LGNL_Services/Business/Markets/Billingsgate+Market/ tours.htm).*
- *The nearest tube station is Canary Wharf.*

SMITHFIELD MEAT MARKET

Smithfield has been a livestock market for over 800 years. In 1852 it was decided to make it a cut meat market only as it was causing mayhem to move livestock through London to Smithfield.

The new market, built by the City of London and designed by Horace Jones, is a wonderful building with its brightly painted ironwork and stunning carved and painted stone dragons.

Pocket Fact 🌉

The names of the pubs around Smithfield reflect the trade that goes on there, including 'The Butcher's Hook and Cleaver' and 'Ye Olde Red Cow'.

After a £70 million refit the market is considered one of the most modern meat markets in Europe with over 85,000 tonnes of meat sold every year. The market is deserted during the day but at 3am it is a hive of activity and the pubs have a special licence to open at this time to serve the traders.

Pocket Tip 🖊

The market and its Buyers Walk are open to all from 3am Monday to Friday, except bank holidays. To see it at its best and with its full range of services and products you should arrive before 7am. The nearest tube stations are Farringdon and Barbican.

NEW COVENT GARDEN MARKET

The original Covent Garden market which was situated just off the Strand dated back to medieval times when the Abbey of Westminster owned 'Convent Garden' and used to sell its surplus produce of fruit and vegetables to the public. The market grew and in 1670 Charles II granted a charter to the Earl of Bedford to hold a regular market. In the 1830s a new dedicated market was built to organise the stalls, but by the 1970s it had become almost impossible for traders and buyers to access the market easily and it was decided to move the market to Nine Elms. The new Covent Garden market sells wonderful and exotic flowers and a huge variety of fruit and vegetables at over 200 outlets.

Pocket Tip 🖊

The market is open from 3am to 11am Monday to Friday and 4am to 10am on Saturdays. The flower market is open Sundays from 4am to 9am. The nearest tube station is Vauxhall.

BOROUGH MARKET

This market is one of the most popular food markets in London selling everything from bread to chillies, including produce from a large number of countries such as Portugal, Argentina and Poland. It is a wonderful place to visit, buying whatever food takes your fancy. The market has been here since the 13th century when traders were moved from the area around London Bridge. In 1755 the market was closed by Parliament but a group of residents bought the patch of land called 'the Triangle' and reopened the market. There are now 130 stalls and the high standard of produce sold is maintained by the 'food quality panel of experts' who ensure the quality and provenance of the produce sold.

Pocket Tip 🖊

Borough market is open on Thursdays, Fridays and Saturdays, with Saturday being busiest after 11am. The sensible shopper gets there between 8am and 10am for the pick of the day. The nearest tube station is London Bridge.

BRIXTON MARKET

This outdoor market is in Electric Avenue and the covered market inside the old 19th-century market arcades is Europe's biggest African Caribbean food market, selling unusual spices and exotic fruit and vegetables and specialist meats and fish.

Pocket Tip 🖊

The market is open Monday to Saturday 8am to 6pm and the nearest tube station is Brixton.

🚗 LONDON'S FOOD SHOPS 🚗

London has a wealth of food shops ranging from large department stores with stunning food halls to small specialist shops focusing on one product. These are some of the best.

Harrods, Knightsbridge

The food halls have to be seen to be believed as they sell everything from biscuits to foie gras to sea urchin. The fish section has a designer display of fish that changes every day. The marble floors and tiled walls are stunning and it is the ideal place to go if you want to buy something that screams London and is good to eat.

Fortnum & Mason, Piccadilly

Go through the oak doors of this oasis of elegant shopping to find fabulous tea, coffee, biscuits, preserves and chocolates on the ground floor and fresh food and wine including cheese and meat on the lower ground floor. The highlights are its world-famous hampers on the first floor and musical biscuit tins and honey from its rooftop beehives.

Pocket Fact 🚲

Don't forget you will be shopping where the Queen and Prince Charles get their food, as Fortnum & Mason has two royal warrants (see p.118).

Paxton & Whitfield, Jermyn Street

This lovely cheesemonger in Jermyn Street was established in 1797. The shop has the most wonderful old-fashioned store front and is said to sell the best Stilton cheese.

Berry Bros & Rudd, St James's Street

This wine shop, which has two royal warrants, was established in 1698 and is still run by the same family. The oldest wine in the shop dates back to 1933 but there is also wine that will not break the bank. Take a walk down St James's just to look at the wonderful shop front.

Neals Yard Dairy, Covent Garden and Borough market

The first store opened in 1979 selling Greek-style yoghurts, crème fraiche and fresh cheeses. It now stocks a selection of cheeses from around 70 producers and its own farm.

Pocket Fact 🌉

Twinings tea shop in the Strand was a coffee shop bought by Thomas Twining in 1706. Competition was fierce between the coffee shops and Thomas decided to offer something different by selling both tea in a cup and dried tea in a packet. Tea had become very popular with the upper classes due to its supposed health benefits. Eventually Thomas was selling more dried tea in packets and this continues in the original shop today.

🚌 FAMOUS FOOD THAT 🚌 ORIGINATED IN LONDON

London is the birthplace for the following classic dishes.

PEACH MELBA

This dessert was created by the French chef Auguste Escoffier in 1893 at the Savoy Hotel for the Australian opera singer Dame Nellie Melba, who regularly performed at the Covent Garden opera house. He served her a dish of poached peach halves on a bed of ice cream with raspberry sauce sitting on an ice sculpture of a swan.

The sandwich

John Montagu, 4th Earl of Sandwich, gave his name to the sandwich, although meat between two slices of bread had been eaten for some time. The Earl was a gambler and so that he did not have to get up from the gaming tables to eat he ordered his servant to bring him meat between two slices of bread as this also allowed him to carry on gambling while he ate with one hand. Other men began to order the 'same as Sandwich' and the name was born.

Jellied eels and pie and mash

Pie and mash and jellied eels are the most traditional food in London and both dishes are bought at the same place, a pie and mash shop. The pie is made with a shortcrust pastry and stewed eels and served with mashed potato and eel liquor sauce or liquor. The liquor is usually made from the water left over from preparing the stewed eels and gets its green colour from the parsley that is added to it.

Jellied eels are chopped eels boiled in a spiced stock that is allowed to cool and set, forming a jelly. They can be eaten hot or cold.

Pocket Tip

The oldest pie and mash shop in London is M. Manze at 87 Tower Bridge Road, where you can eat in or order a takeaway.

Eels were plentiful in the filthy river Thames in the 18th century and were nutritious and cheap food for the working classes. Traditionally, the shops had tiled walls with wooden bench seats and white marble tabletops. Pie and mash shops are still popular today.

🚗 TRADITIONAL RESTAURANTS 🚗

London has a number of traditional restaurants where you can find typically English food such as steak and kidney pie, steamed puddings, roast beef, and fish and chips.

BEST FOR TRADITIONAL ENGLISH DISHES

Rules, Maiden Lane

The oldest restaurant in London was established by Thomas Rule in 1798 and has been owned by only three families, the Rules,

Bells and now John Mayhew. The restaurant has a reputation for serving traditional English food, including steak and kidney pudding, steak and oyster pie and game meats such as deer and pigeon. It also serves traditional English puddings such as golden syrup pudding and steamed chocolate pudding. Rules has a long history of feeding the great and the good including Charles Dickens, H. G. Wells, Laurence Olivier, Clark Gable and Charlie Chaplin.

Pocket Fact ⚓

The collection of drawings, paintings and cartoons of the famous patrons that adorn the walls were described by John Betjeman as 'unique and irreplaceable, and part of literary and theatrical London'.

Simpsons-in-the-Strand

This beautiful wood-panelled restaurant began in 1828 as a chess and coffee house called the 'The Grand Cigar Divan'. To avoid disturbing the chess players, roasted meat was served on silver domed trolleys and this continues today. In 1848 the owner Reiss joined with John Simpson to expand the premises and it was renamed 'Simpsons Grand Cigar Divan'. In 1898 it was bought by Richard D'Oyly Carte for the Savoy Hotel and when it reopened in 1904 after redevelopment it was renamed Simpsons-in-the-Strand. The restaurant serves roast beef, lamb and game in season and all the meat is carved at the diner's table.

Pocket Tip 📍

Simpsons-in-the-Strand offers courses on master carving. For more details go to the restaurant's website (www.simpsonsinthes-trand.co.uk/classes.php).

BEST RESTAURANTS FOR FISH

Wiltons, 55 Jermyn Street

This restaurant, with its elegant decorative features and green gingham-uniformed waitresses, started as a stall in 1742, selling oysters, shrimps and cockles. It has been at its present premises since 1984 and is known for its wild fish, shellfish, and game in season and meat dishes.

Pocket Fact

In 1942, when a bomb landed on St James's church near to the restaurant, the owner, Mrs Leal, became concerned for her safety and decided to close the restaurant. Olaf Hambro was sitting at the oyster bar and on a whim asked that the restaurant be added to his bill. Olaf reopened the restaurant a week later and the family still own it today.

J. Sheekey, 32–34 St Martins Court

This wood-panelled seafood restaurant and oyster bar dates back to 1896 and with the elegantly dressed doorman in his top hat does excellent fish and chips and a wide variety of seafood. The restaurant is often frequented by actors including Keira Knightly and Ewan McGregor as it is close to London's theatre district. The pictures of many of its famous clients hang on the walls.

Pocket Fact

The Beefeaters have their own pub called 'The Tower of London Club' where the walls are lined with photographs of celebrities and politicians including Johnny Depp, Matt Damon and Barack Obama, who have all had their picture taken with the Beefeaters.